THE SHAPE OF SHIT
TO COME

THE SHAPE OF SHIT TO COME

STEVE LOWE AND ALAN McARTHUR

The Friday Project
An imprint of HarperCollinsPublishers
77–85 Fulham Palace Road
Hammersmith, London W6 8JB
www.harpercollins.co.uk

First published in Great Britain by The Friday Project in 2012
This edition published 2014

1

Alan McArthur and Steve Lowe assert their moral right to
be identified as the authors of this work

A catalogue record for this book
is available from the British Library

978-0-00-758640-0

Typeset by Palimpsest Book Production Limited
Falkirk, Stirlingshire

Printed and bound in Great Britain by
Clays Ltd, St Ives plc

MIX
Paper from
responsible sources
FSC
www.fsc.org
FSC™ C007454

Find out more about HarperCollins and the environment at
www.harpercollins.co.uk/green

THE SHAPE OF SHIT TO COME

INTRODUCTION

Are you ready to be innovated?

Are you ready for a world of kids making their own pets with gene-splicing kits? Or food that comes in packets that talk to you about how to cook the contents? While geeky types graft robot limbs onto themselves in a bid to become immortal before blasting off to their holiday homes in space?

You're not ready. Don't fool yourself.

The future was meant to come with a capital F – the genetic enhancements, the moon bases, the supercomputers killing all the humans . . . aaaaaargh! – but then it didn't arrive. But a whole host of techy advances currently in development hell mean that this time, more than any other time, the future is coming.

Are you ready for the people trying to clone mammoths from frozen DNA? People you actually know – friends of yours – having sex with robots? The wearable computers?

Maybe you are ready for wearable computers. We'll give you that one.

This book started with idle curiosity about what was taking shape in the world. We suspected something was going down with technology. But a few peeks round the corner rapidly became a series of moments – shared here – of going: fucking hell – *really?* Our eyes widened, in fear and excitement, and stayed wide for ages.

As it transpires, out there on the fringes of public consciousness, nerds made rich as Croesus by the Internet are joining messianic scientists and military researchers in bringing some mind-bending things to pass. iPhones aren't even the half of it. The mad professors have got the keys to the genetically modified sweetshop. And we all know what that means. Except we don't – which is the point.

And while we're out front in the shop, trying to get our heads round the genetically modified sweets, they're in the back turning themselves into multi-bodied super-strength cyborgs with spooky telepathic powers. It's like they're always one step ahead of us.

In this super new world, it is hard to stay grounded. Even renowned physicists writing pop-science round-ups of current developments will veer madly between sober scientific inquiry and saying how it is our nailed-on 'destiny' to become 'The Gods of Mythology', and liberally pepper their writing with references to deities and superheroes. But this stuff is so nuts, it is no wonder the scientists start believing they are Thor (during the writing of this book, we too have occasionally had moments of thinking we are Thor . . . we actually might be Thor – can two people be Thor?).

In this book we sceptically scour the labs, the theories, the freaky cults, the Internet mega-corporateers who all ride scooters around, indoors . . . and ask questions like: don't all the people who go to space come back mad? Are GM crops such a headfuck because the people who make them are such utter bastards, yet the people who oppose them are such hippy mentalists? And also, how long will it be before we hear the tragic question: 'Mummy? Why is Daddy sleeping in the robot's room?'

Some of what is happening promises great things for humanity. Some of it promises the end of humanity. So it's worth paying attention. Otherwise we will leave our fate in the hands of adults who ride scooters indoors. They ride around on scooters indoors, but hold in their hands the power to change human nature itself.

What have we done?

CHAPTER 1: GENES

The mouse that did not roar, but instead made another surprising animal noise

This was no ordinary mouse. In January 2012, Japanese scientists announced they had genetically engineered a new kind of mouse. A mouse unlike other mice. Those mice squeaked. Not this mouse. This mouse went where no other mouse had, sonically speaking, gone before. This mouse tweeted, like a bird.

Lead researcher Arikuni Uchimura of Osaka University's well-named School of Frontier Biosciences said of the process that led to this fantastical creation: 'We have cross-bred the genetically modified mice for generations to see what would happen.'

That's right: they wanted to see what would happen. And what did happen? A mouse tweeted like a bird. It's fucked up.

Biotech – which is short for biotechnology, which is short for biological technology, which is not short for anything – is running wild. The building blocks of nature are a minefield. And the minefield is on fire. Not a day goes by without a headline like 'Genetic breakthrough could slow – or halt – the ageing process' or 'Why hating brussels sprouts could be in your

DNA' or 'Glowing Cats Shed Light On AIDS'. (I deliberately didn't look at that last story – preferring my own reverie.)

The mysteries of life itself are being unravelled before our eyes. Think of the ramifications, and also the implications. We are gaining the ability to mess with human genes – possibly changing characteristics, for good or ill, for generations to come.

Some call this playing God. But why should we not play God? Why should He have all the fun? Maybe He was wrong in having the mice squeak and birds tweet. Maybe it's time to mix that whole game right up. From now on, maybe we should treat mice that merely squeak with the disdain they deserve.

But who gets to play God? Many bleeding-edge geneticists have a sort of punk-rock DIY libertarian aesthetic that favours posting gene codes on the Internet so anyone can knock up new strains in the garage. It's a world of out-there ideas. Veteran future-watcher and renowned Princeton physicist Freeman Dyson believes the biotech revolution will be fun, and educative: he believes we should welcome gene-splicing kits in the homeplace. He even joyfully envisages biotech kids' games 'where you give the child some eggs and seeds and a kit for writing the genomes and see what comes out'.

See what comes out? *See what comes out?* I'll tell you what'll 'come out' of giving children the power to bend nature: a catalogue of horrors, that's what. Jurassic Park? Jurassic Fucking Reindeer-Shark, more like.

What can we learn from the really weird animals?

Like latterday Dr Dolittles, life scientists seem to want to talk to the animals, by making animals that talk. Or at least, animals that glow in the dark.

Life science has acquired an odd public reputation – forever synonymous with importing rabbits and mice on ferries for kicks. But the life scientists are certainly getting up to some pretty intriguing experiments. Most experiments are, when all is said and done, tedious as all hell. But these are *experiments*. It's like they're on E, but with the 'E' standing for 'Experiment'. Or 'Extreme Shit Being Done With Animals'.

Scientists in the Netherlands have injected cows with the protein lactoferrin derived from humans. Found in breast milk and tears, this little bit of *Homo sapiens* would allegedly help boost cows' immune systems. (Cows swimming with human tears? It's already happened.) Goats on a farm run by Utah State University have been genetically modified with spider genes so they produce silk in their milk. You think it's milk, but no . . . it's silk! Or, at least, silky milk (milky silk?). Then there is ANDi, the world's first transgenic monkey ('transgenic' means combining genes).

ANDi, whose name contains 'DNA' backwards, was born following experiments conducted by researchers at the Oregon Health and Science University. ANDi was no common or garden transgenic monkey: he was a transgenic monkey with some jellyfish DNA spliced into him. That is, jellyfish DNA was cut and pasted – literally – into monkey DNA. If you hold a torch up to ANDi, he glows a bit green.

So on some levels these animal experiments seem quite mind-bending, and on others a bit silly. In choosing to create a chimerical mythic creature anew the scientists eschewed classical models like the Chimera itself – lion, goat and snake – in favour of a slightly fluorescent monkey. (Of course, slightly fluorescent monkeys could easily lead on to slightly fluorescent human beings: not just useful for finding people in the dark, but also fun in the bedchamber.)

What the scientists love most, though, is fucking up mice. Everyone remembers the most famous transgenic mouse, the so-called Vacanti mouse (named after its inventor, the MIT professor Charles Vacanti), burdened with what appeared to be a ruddy great human ear on its back. This mouse had a ruddy great ear on its back, but couldn't even hear through it. So that's odd. In a full-page *New York Times* ad one anti-testing group labelled this striking image 'an actual photo of a genetically engineered mouse with a human ear on its back' – which was actually incorrect. The 'ear' was just cartilage grown into the shape of a human ear, although you can sort of see how this misapprehension might have taken hold, what with it looking like a mouse with an ear on its fucking back.

Anyway, transgenic mice are everywhere. In 2007, biologists in Cleveland conjured up a so-called 'super-mouse' that could run six kilometres without pausing for breath or sustenance. That's one hell of a useful mouse. It could carry very small packages or messages on paper. Hang on, there's e-mail for that. It's useful. It'll come to me . . .

So-called 'smart mice' have been engineered at Princeton. Altered with an extra gene that boosts the neurotransmitter NMDA (N.B., not MDMA – that would be a different experiment entirely), the mice get a brainpower boost and outperform ordinary mice in various mouse-cleverness tests. Sadly, they also scare more easily. Meanwhile, Larry Young at Emory University transferred a gene from the monogamous prairie vole into the hitherto promiscuous lab mouse – and created monogamous mice. So there's *a lot* of stuff going on with mice. Less shagging around, in one instance.

But this is not just mutants for mutants' sake (not always). Some of these experiments on animals are showing humanity a brave new dawn in the here and now. Geneticists also based in Cleveland are producing transgenic mosquitoes that do not carry malaria, which in Cayman Island trials have started squeezing out mosquitoes that do. So that's good, because malaria is bad.

Then there's using animals to develop stuff useful for humans in a more direct way – by means of xenotransplantation: the breeding of animals for harvesting organs to transplant into humans. Renowned fertility expert and television star Lord Robert Winston is working on breeding GM pigs whose hearts can be transplanted into humans.

The heart of a pig is about the same size as the heart of a man. If liberally covered in human protein, it may be accepted by the human body. And, okay, it sounds wrong – putting the heart of a pig into a man. But is it wrong? Clearly it is. But is it? It's the heart of a pig. But they're putting it into a man. Is that wrong? There are risks for safety in all of this (no, really) – for example, of contracting animal viruses. Plus it might make you go off sausages, which just isn't worth the risk. (Maybe this is why Robert Winston is so twinkly eyed on the telly: he has just been bending nature on the sly.)

Even the supermice could have human applications. The Cleveland mice lived longer, ate more without getting fat and had more sex; some humans might also want to live longer, eat more without getting fat and have more sex. Could not supermice lead to genetically enhanced super*men*? The researchers said that was not the aim of the project, before pointing out that humans do also possess this highly active gene for an enzyme called phosphoenolpyruvate carboxykinase (PEPCK). 'But this is not something that you'd do to a human,' said Professor Richard Hanson of Cleveland's Case Western Reserve University.

He has not even thought about it. No way. Not even once. Going down in history as the creator of a new breed of superbeings has never even begun to occur to him. 'It's completely wrong,' he added.

(He can't stop thinking about it.)

Anyway, one group of scientists is making mice monogamous, while another is making them randy. And that is what experimenting on animals is all about.

We want to help you overcome your genes

Many are calling the twenty-first century the century of biology. Mainly it's the biologists calling it that. But they do have a point. The century began with a bang, biologically speaking, with the rough completion of the Human Genome Project (HGP) – 'biology's Apollo landing' – in 2000. Large-scale messing with your actual humans at a genetic level came one huge step closer with the mapping of the human genome (all the genetic info in a person), aka the Road Atlas of Man.

It was a hell of a thing. Even just reading out the entire code (some 3 billion DNA base pairs, or 23,000 genes) would take about twelve years – so don't do that. This achievement was announced with great fanfare by then US-president Bill Clinton, a fervent supporter of the efforts – and he had more to fear from genetics than most, having totalled his presidency by spilling some seed on an intern's dress. 'We are learning the language in which God created Life,' he said. (About the HGP, not while he was getting off with Monica Lewinsky.) (Although maybe then too.)

So what have we learnt? We already know that cauliflowers contain more genes than humans. So having lots of genes isn't everything; no one is claiming cauliflowers have anything approaching human consciousness (there is nothing cruel about cauliflower cheese). But mainly what we have learnt is that we still have much to learn. We have mapped the human genome, but we don't know how most of it works. We are trying to find the secrets written in the DNA. It's like runes, man.

The HGP cost $3bn, which is a lot of money. But the costs are rapidly falling for having your own genetic code sequenced (it currently costs over £2,000). So you are now able to have a much better idea of how you will die (cancer, Hodgkinson's, Parkinson's . . .). So that's nice. But then, there is also the prospect of targeted medicine. As the price of mapping genes comes down, you could get drugs optimised for your particularities (people respond to drugs differently); so-called pharmacogenetics. You could even treat an illness before you get it. Treating diseases you don't yet have – it's the future.

Mapping everyone's genome raises questions of privacy, of course, and who gets access to the info. For employers, genetic discrimination could become a new type of discrimination to replace some of the old ones, like skin colour. Or the insurance industry could refuse to insure those at genetic risk. And it goes without saying the world should always applaud any new opportunities for the insurance industry to turn a profit; they are our friends.

Clearly some genes have particular purposes – like the ones that make mice horny. Scientists are keen to work out what the various human genes do, and claim to have isolated numerous genes which supposedly make up our personalities, including the gluttony gene, the long-life gene, the psychopath gene, the susceptible-to-flu gene, the genius gene, the infidelity gene, the suicide gene and even the liberal gene. Imagine having all of those. It would be one hell of a ride, albeit ultimately tragic.[1]

These efforts bring the fear that we will not just muss with genes to banish illness, but to positively engineer in boosts to intelligence or looks, or even personality types. Designer babies could be created by gene therapy – inserting genes into the cells of an embryo – encouraging or discouraging certain predispositions. This might be used to phase out cancer, or it might be used to phase out liberals.

Anyone trying to do either will face difficulties. Genes, unsurprisingly enough, work together in ways of fiendish complexity. Boosting up one seemingly positive gene might cause some unwanted side-effects; the Cleveland supermice were great lovers, yes, but were also highly

[1] In the near future, scientists also expect to isolate the down-in-one gene, the too-small-teeth gene, the Catholic-priest gene, the stands-slightly-too-close gene and, of course, the looks-a-bit-like-a-waiter-even-though-they're-not-a-waiter gene.

aggressive. 'Why this is the case, we are not really sure,' admitted Professor Hanson.

But for some, the potential profits are unignorable. In 2009, a Los Angeles clinic – LA Fertility Institutes – run by controversial IVF pioneer Dr Jeff Steinberg, offered would-be parents the chance to select their kid's hair and eye colours – making sure to offer no money back guarantee. 'I would not say this is a dangerous road,' Dr Steinberg said. 'It's an uncharted road.'

But a road that is uncharted is, by definition, a dangerous road because it is uncharted. You do not know whether it is a safe road or one that is beset by marauding blonde-haired superchildren who see you as a source of cheap fuel. That's the main worry here. And one that saw public opinion force Steinberg to, at least temporarily, withdraw the service. We weren't ready for the master race quite yet.

Strange about the Cleveland mice, though: you'd have thought a mouse that was getting it that often would be pretty relaxed. But that's genetic complexity for you.

Is all this genetics just eugenics under another name?

There is a question underlying all this genetical jiggery-pokery and that question is this: is all this genetics just eugenics under another name? Stamping out impurities in the human gene pool? Many are touchy about this kind of thing. If we did manage to phase a 'psychopath gene' out of the gene pool, would that not be a good thing? Or are you some kind of psychopath fan? Then again, mastering nature to breed a race of supermen: isn't this just a teeny bit Nazi? It does sound a bit Nazi. It's probably the words 'master', 'race', 'breed' and 'supermen'.

The word genetics replaced eugenics as the name for the field after certain mid-twentieth-century embarrassments. The word 'eugenics' is derived from the Greek for 'good in birth' and was coined by Victorian polymath Francis Galton who believed inherited physical problems caused much misery. If we bred from the best specimens and made people happier and cleverer, life would be generally better. But the 'best' of humanity, it turned out, were the gentryfolk like Galton while the 'worst' were the urban poor, who drank and swore and wore clogs and suchlike. (He wrote some *hilarious* blogs about 'chav scum').

And it's not just Nazis who have been a bit Nazi about all this. By 1927, many US states had eugenics laws permitting them to sterilise people deemed 'imbeciles'. They rowed back from – but thoroughly debated – the idea of gassing people. In Britain, in 1913, the Liberal Government passed the Mental Deficiency Act which early supporters, like Winston Churchill, had initially hoped would sanction sterilisation of 'the feeble minded and insane classes'. The last time the USA sterilised someone was . . . 1972. (On US soil, that is; attaching electrodes to Iraqi nads doesn't count.) In 1995, good old 'socialist' China passed a law limiting the right of low-IQ people to reproduce.

So is all gene-related work essentially 'eugenics' under another name? Well, yes. But there is clearly a difference between hindering the spread of cancer and hindering the spread of alleged imbeciles.

We have moved on from Justice Oliver Wendell Holmes's jolly pronouncement about the twenties US laws: 'We want people who are healthy, good-natured, emotionally stable, sympathetic, and smart. We do not want idiots, imbeciles, paupers, and criminals.'

I mean, he's right in a way: who does want idiots, imbeciles, paupers and criminals? Not me. Not after last time. But most would now agree that fascistically stopping people breeding is not really helping anyone and the USA for one has a far more enlightened attitude to imbeciles – sometimes even making them president.

But trying not to slip into being a teeny bit fascist remains a big issue with genetics. Most are pretty careful to avoid muddying the waters, though this cannot really be said for James Watson, the American genetics legend who, with Francis Crick, discovered DNA in a Cambridge pub in 1952 and now runs one of America's leading scientific research institutions. In 2004, pondering genetic engineering's potential uses, this figurehead wondered if there was any harm in breeding 'pretty girls' (he *really likes* pretty girls).

More controversial was his contention that being 'really stupid' is 'a disease' that we could also try banishing from the gene pool. Still, at least he wasn't being racist or anything. Oh, no, hang on . . .

He also claimed that black people were less intelligent than white, which definitely sounds like the sort of thing that people call racist. Yes, he did acknowledge that modern science claimed all human groups were intellectually equal, but 'people who have to deal with black employees find this not true'.

Man alive.

Transhuman express

Of course, your genes do not determine everything. Anyone who thinks individual genes mechanistically decide our fates is onto a loser. Have they not even seen *Trading Places*? 'It's a miracle – I've got legs! I can walk!' Great days.

But neither do your genes determine nothing. It's tricky. What more greatly determines our characters: our intrinsic, genetically inherited natures, or the conditions in which we are nurtured? We could perhaps call this debate one of 'nature versus nurture'. It's a snappy phrase that really should catch on.

Even so, genetic enhancement (boosting ourselves at the genetic level) is one of the ways some starry-eyed Silicon Valley zealots, the world's newest elite, believe humanity will push past its current incarnation – transgressing our limits to become transhuman, or even eventually post-human. Genetically enriched – or GenRich, to sound more techy – humans could have better intellectual and physical capabilities. Oh yes, and they will not have to die.

As well as genetic engineering, the transhumanists look to emergent techniques like stem cell research and growing replacement organs in the lab. Stem cell research offers the possibility of potentially banishing many diseases (Parkinson's, cancer, diabetes, Alzheimer's, multiple sclerosis) by getting diseased parts of the body to repair themselves from stem cells, the cells from which other cells develop. (It also freaks out the religious right, so it's the gift that keeps on giving.) The transhumanists bundle this all in with medical nanotechnology (of which more later . . . it means 'small technology') to create a vision of the future where the human body's ageing processes can be halted, or bits of us renewed (or even robotised). Basically, they reckon they can live for ever.

There is even a World Transhumanist Association which holds conferences called things like 'Living For Ever'. One leading transhumanist is Natasha Vita-More, the glamorous chair of Humanity+, a libertarian group dedicated to utilising everything it possibly can to stay trim. She is so committed to living longer that she changed her name to Vita-More. Probably born in the early 1950s, she is utilising all technologies available to stay young-looking – yes, currently that does mean a hell of a lot of plastic surgery. And changing your name.

'I have never stopped dancing, it simply has taken on different rhythms and steps. And we need to dance with our ideas, words and pen — which transhumanists do take seriously,' she says. And why not? This is the sort of talk that transhumanists talk.

Aubrey de Grey sounds like an Oscar Wilde character and is, by coincidence, also obsessed with not ageing. This 49-year-old London-born/California-based 'biogerontologist' has the massive beard of the self-conscious eccentric – a massive beard that ironically makes him appear far older than he is, which seems a bit counterproductive to say the least. His foundation is called Strategies for Engineered Negligible Senescence (SENS) and suggests that if we get rid of the things that people generally die of in old age, then we will not die.

'There is a tendency to think there is some sort of inevitability about ageing,' he says, correctly.

But humans could become one of those creatures who

hardly age at all, like lobsters – only better. De Grey envisages a world of humans living for thousands of years, whose only cause of death is suicide or murder. And no-one shaves (not sure if that's integral).

De Grey's efforts have been partly funded by PayPal co-founder and billionaire Peter Thiel, a strongly right-wing libertarian and leading light among the so-called Paypal Mafia, a Silicon Valley clique of billionaires who got in early on creaming off a small amount of money from a great many Internet purchases and now love them-selves and future-science possibly overmuch.

But why does de Grey want to live so long? Isn't a standard life long enough anyway? In an interview with the *Washington Post*, de Grey proffered his reasons. 'So many women. So much time.'

Hey ladies. Come and get it. Come and get some of beardy Aubrey! Don't rush. He has all the time you need. Oh yeah. I'm a love train, baby. A beardy love train.

Let's assume, though, that the transhumanists are right to some degree and technologies arrive that actually work in boosting human capacities. If some get boosted and not others, is that fair? Not really.

Many transhumanists might say they are not bothered about being fair. Life's not fair, so what's the point in even starting with that shit? But others are properly fearful of a divided future of the enhanced versus the non-enhanced leading to a rather regrettable enslavement/genocide scenario (or competing tribal subspecies perpetually battling for supremacy).

It goes without saying that the already moneyed will be first in the queue for any enhancements. So perhaps we should picture this future world as an insanely exclusive, insanely tribal club scene, with door staff checking out the size of your genetic wad: 'Your legs are crap and your IQ's piss and you're not going to live for 120 years. You're not coming in.' And then they kill you.

Should we really be worried about this? Well, when asked what his greatest fear was for the future of humanity, Stephen Hawking replied: 'It is over genetic engineering. It should soon be possible dramatically to increase the intelligence and life span of a few individuals. They and their offspring could become a master race. Evolution pays no regard to social justice. It was not fair on the Neanderthals they were replaced by modern humans.'

Remember, this guy was right about time.

Attack of the cloned neanderthals

Cloning humans might be the sexy side of genetics that gets in lots of Hollywood films, but it raises a whole host of thorny issues. What if your clone is more interesting than you? Is it okay to clone someone without their permission? And what if two clones took a shine to each other: should there be a lawful impediment to the two of them having a civil partnership?

There are also the moral issues. And the fact it's fiendishly difficult. And illegal.

Animal cloning has been with us for years, of course. The breakthrough clone was Polly the Sheep. Yes: Polly the Sheep. Everyone knows about Dolly, but Polly, who followed soon after, was actually more significant, but was eclipsed by Dolly's absurd fame.

Polly had human therapeutic protein genes inserted. So did Molly (yeah, there was a Molly; don't mention Golli, everyone's trying to move on from that whole debacle). So Polly had human genes, whereas headline-hogger Dolly the Sheep (named after Dolly Parton: FACT) was just a sheep. And a sickly one at that.

Dolly was born in July 1996 – and put down in 2003, at the age of six (half the normal lifespan of a sheep). She was suffering from a lung disease generally only common in much older sheep, and was obese, and had arthritis.

Some said this was because she was a clone (no shit); others said it was the strange circumstances of her upbringing, blaming the parents, in this case Ian Wilmut and Keith Campbell of the Roslin Institute, the chaps who popped the DNA nucleus from the cell of an adult sheep into an egg cell. Yet others still said that she was a victim of her 'celebrity lifestyle', stressed out from all the photo opps and prodding.

I have to admit that I go quite strongly with the celebrity lifestyle theory. I knew Dolly a bit when she was on the scene and I can still recall her now, mired in her own sleaze and degradation, compromising hint-of-teat photos splashed all over *Farming News*, her phone hacked by the *Independent* . . .

. . . falling out of the back of taxis, laughing with the paparazzi even as they hungrily consumed her decline . . .

. . . those sex tapes . . .

. . . at the end, a Norma Desmond figure, hanging round the lab with the blinds drawn: 'It's just the test tubes that got small . . .'

So: they can clone sheep. Human cloning is still off the cards – illegal in all countries of the world. This, at least, is a line that shall not be crossed. Or is it? Geneva-based alien-loving sex cult The Raëlians claimed in 2002 that a cloned baby had been born to a Dutch lesbian couple the previous day, which led to headlines like CNN's 'Dutch lesbian gives birth to cloned baby'. But we should probably take the idea that Dutch lesbians have given birth to a cloned baby with a pinch of salt. (No, really.) [2]

But cloning animals is cool, and seemingly involves a race to clone the animal with the weirdest name: the gaur (a type of ox), the mouflon (a rare sheep), and the banteng (a type of Japanese cattle) have all allegedly been cloned. It's not impossible that they made those names up. That's the sort of shit that scientists could easily get away with. 'The, er, banteng? [snigger] It's, uh . . . Japanese cattle from, uh, Japan . . . Honestly – I've got receipts.'

Meanwhile, scientists in Australia have been trying to clone a woolly mammoth from frozen DNA. Scientists have also seriously debated the ethics of cloning Neanderthals (who are not covered by the current laws banning human cloning).

Cloned Neanderthals hunting cloned woolly mammoths: this would definitely be an achievement of sorts. Wrong,

[2] These days, the Raëlians appear more focused on other matters like promoting sex-positive feminism, including topless rights for all and waiting for our alien ancestors, the Elohim, to arrive and save us. A planned 2008 'International Orgasm Day' was to bring around 250 people to simultaneous public orgasm either by masturbation or sexual intercourse to help achieve world peace, but was cancelled at the last minute, presumably causing a few disappointed faces.

21

clearly. But the sort of wrong you might pay good money to see.

It has also been mooted – technological leaps willing – that by approximating it from human and Neanderthal DNA, we might be able to recreate the DNA of the missing link betwixt ape and man and bring it to life. Then there's the dodo – which, if they do bring it back, will mean binning the saying 'dead as', perhaps replacing it with 'as fucked up as a brought back to life dodo'. And, of course, using what we know about particular dinosaur DNA to conjure up a 'generalised dinosaur'. Bring that lot forth and we've got one hell of a swinging party. Jurassic Reindeer-Shark? Jurassic Park, more like.

So genetics could make the future one big mad menagerie of fucked-up shit. It's also even suggested we could bring back dead poets, scientists and Elvis (it would certainly be a Comeback Special worthy of the name).

Then truly shall we be gods. Quite weird gods, pissing about doing pretty odd stuff to mice and mammoths. But gods nonetheless.

CHAPTER 2: ROBOTS

Does not include batteries

Robots that act passably human are imminent. Sad to say that, as with the Internet, many people's first response to this revolutionary new technology will be: 'I could shag that.'

Out there, right now, some early adopters are already at it. One US company run by former construction worker Scott Maclean has been producing naughty robots – or rather, slightly mechanised sex-dolls – since 2004.

Maclean has satisfied customers' requests for custom-made look-alikes of Angelina Jolie and Pamela Anderson. Another request was less predictable: one woman wanted her robot to look like Eurovision host Graham Norton.

So yes. The human race has produced its first Graham Norton robot sex-dolls. In *our* lifetimes. We should be, well . . . not proud exactly. But we should probably feel *something*.

The sex robots are coming. And so are the war robots. Lots of other useful robots are already here, doing the hoovering and cleaning the sewers. So are we on the verge of a time where finally – finally, after all the false robot dawns – robots start doing loads of our shitty jobs for us? And loads of our tricky jobs, like surgery? And all the other jobs?

In Asia, where attitudes to robots are ones of great enthusiasm, they are already making inroads into loads of areas of society. But will the robots get ideas above their stations and wipe out the illogical old humans in a big fuck-off robot takeover scenario?

The word 'robot' was coined by the Czech writer Karel Čapek – from *robota* meaning serf labour – for a cautionary 1920 play called *R.U.R.* (Rossum's Universal Robots). The title refers to a fictional factory which pumps out artificial humanoids who initially work for mankind without complaint. Things take a turn for the worse when they rise up and wipe out all humanity. So it's been a motif from the start.

But who or what will be in at the finish? Robots? I expect so.

The robots are not coming! The robots are not coming! The robots are already here

Different parts of the world have very varied attitudes to robotics. Asian societies generally believe that the more robots advance, the better this is for humans. Western societies generally believe the more robots advance, the more likely they are to rise up and kill us all in our beds, dashing out our brains as we sleep. Aaaaaargh! This is a fundamental difference of opinion as regards robots.

Japan and South Korea are engaged in a race to be the most robotic (with China coming up on the rails). South Korea is currently constructing a theme park called Robot Land. That's a theme park for people to see robots, not a place for robots to relax.

The theme of Robot Land is robots. Very much so. An hour outside Seoul, Robot Land promises attractions like an aquarium full of robot fish, movie sets from *Minority Report* and *I, Robot*, a giant robot arm that flings you around, Vegas-style robot shows and even 'boxer-bot' fight nights (hopefully complete with the press conference brawl with mike stands). There is even a water park, which seems a bit off; you wouldn't have thought robots would even like water, what with being electric.

South Korea also has robot guards patrolling prison perimeters; robot screws on wheels, with smiles etched onto their 'faces' supposedly making them more 'humane and friendly', but actually just making them look freakier than that by far.

Throughout Korean society, a mechanical underclass is taking over many of the dirty jobs like being a soldier or a waiter, or a teacher. By 2013, every class in the land is promised a three-foot tall robot teaching assistant who bowls around the classroom on wheels, speaking in English and dancing to music. Teachers dancing: that's a bit embarrassing (although it would probably be quite good at robotic dancing). And what sort of kids will they end up with, reared by robots? (Pro-robot ones if the robots have got anything to do with it.) (Which they have.)

Japan, meanwhile, has a robot factory entirely staffed by robots. The FANUC Robotics factory can operate for 53 days without human intervention, pumping out more robots without the need for meals or heat or ventilation or lines of speed or anything. Robots making robots, for weeks at a time, without pause: is this wise? It doesn't sound wise.

Then there is the 'guard dragon' robot for the home; a four-legged robot that can sense smoke and alert its owners to a smouldering fire via a howl or a text message. Yes, a dog can howl, but can a dog text?

There are also the robot chefs that can make a range of meals from a set menu, the robot avatars that cover for you in the office[3] and Toyota's robot that plays the violin – often considered the most emotive of all the instruments (although not the way this guy plays it). Other robots have mastered trumpets and trombones, so watch out for the full robot orchestra. If the robots do take over, a strident classical overture – some Wagner, say – is exactly the sort of dramatic flourish they'd be into.

Japan is also leading the way in empathetic robots – which does sound like a contradiction in terms, and possibly is. But that does not bother the Japanese. There is a robotic bear that cures snoring, an emotional robot pillow and cuddly robot companions providing comfort and solace for the elderly. One cute robotic seal called Paro was even selected by *Guinness World Records* as the world's most soothing robot. How could they even claim to be objective about this? Surely one person's soothing robot is not the same as another's, moving the whole thing into dangerously subjective waters.

Japan's elderly can also get about aided by battery-powered robotic pants. These are designed to help people with mobility problems move without the need for human

[3] The makers of these robots, as clever as the bots are, can get carried away. One of the developers of the office avatars, the QB office-bot, claimed: 'Someone recently came to the office asking for me, and a colleague told them they had just seen me. But actually it was the robot they had just seen, I was still at home.' Ha! Brilliant! That didn't happen.

assistance, picking up traces of the brain's signals to nerves on the skin, and helping move the limbs accordingly. Battery-powered robot pants: is that wise? It doesn't sound wise. (Have they not seen *The Wrong Trousers*?)

The Japanese persist in incubating the robots even after one humanoid security robot, following an alleged 'malfunction', attacked Prime Minister Junichiro Koizumi, taking a swing and firing smoke at him during a factory visit. Most people would take this as a sign, but, in fact, they just keep making the robots bigger and more powerful. So do the Koreans. Indeed, these two pre-eminent robot nations are in competition to make the biggest giant robot of them all, feverishly trying to churn out yet bigger and bigger and more powerful bots.

First Japan built a 59 – foot-high giant robot – a life-size replica of the anime legend Gundam – in the city of Odaiba, with another equivalent one being constructed in Kobe.

But these will both be dwarfed by South Korea's plans for a 364-foot-tall Taekwon V to tower over the Robot Land theme park. Stick that, Japan – get a load of our robot!

Is Japan likely to let their ancient rivals reign victorious in the giantest giant robot race? No. They will continue making ever more gargantuan robots until they black out the very sky and bring fear and terror to the quivering peoples below.

All fine stuff, except this does rather resemble a sci-fi parable which ends with the giant robots coming to life and going on an epic trampling rampage until both nations are unfortunately reduced to tear-stained dust – thus providing a salutary lesson for all mankind about the inadvisability of conjuring up really, really big robots.

This may not happen. Let's hope it doesn't. But they are kind of asking for it by building all these giant robots. The idiots.

Robots in the house

Clearly robots have not happened as envisaged in the futuristic fantasies of yore. Here in the West, we do not appear to be surrounded by domestic robot slaves and are not joined in the workplace by spooky near-human androids. There have been delays. Philip K. Dick's *Do Androids Dream of Electric Sheep?* – the novel which became *Blade Runner* – was originally set in 1992. As you may recall, 1992 was the year of the Maastricht Treaty and Brian May's solo single 'Too Much Love Will Kill You'. But not near-human replicant serfs suddenly breaking free and being hunted down by bounty hunters in a fictional-philosophical inquiry into empathy. Not that.

No one who has seen any of the current robots, in all their stumbling whirring glory, can be too terrified that they are about to break free, or take over, or even successfully make some tea. In the main, these prototype humanoids tottering about their labs are highly expensive idiots who fall over all the time.

Most chores, like washing up, are sadly still beyond most robots. Anyone seeking to employ current modern-day robot helpers for such purposes would face a great many chipped cafetière pots. (Is a dishwasher a robot, though? This is the sort of question we must get our heads around.)

But we do have robot hoovers: for £200, you can now buy the Roomba robot vacuum cleaner, a large disc which scoots around the floor sucking up dirt, produced by pioneering US company iRobot. iRobot co-founder Helen Greiner recalled people's preconceptions before the product launch: 'Focus groups imagined it would look like the Terminator pushing a vacuum cleaner and told us they would not accept such machines in their homes.' Which seems a fair judgement. Who wants the Terminator crashing round their house?

In Germany, they have robots maintaining the sewers. This seems like tempting fate. If robots are going to take over then coming up out of the sewers is exactly the sort of dramatic touch they'll be looking for. They're called Autonomous Sewer Robots. Perhaps the word autonomous worries you? It should: it means they can do whatever the hell they fucking well like down there.

In a similarly worrying move, the University of the West of England has produced a 'release and forget' bot that powers itself by 'eating' flies. It's called Lord of the Flies. No it isn't. It's called EcoBot II. It 'shits' little waste pellets. Then there's the so-called Vampire Bot, a tiny fuel cell that powers itself on blood. It's based in Texas, but a team of Japanese scientists is working on a similar project. For fuck's sake – don't *help* them drink our blood!

Anyway, out in the real world the cost of robot workers has fallen sharply against the cost of actual worker workers. Amazon's warehouses are run by short orange robots designed by Kiva Systems – a bit like Ooompa Loompas, but robots (they don't sing.

Well, they might – I don't actually know). Scientists are even looking at replacing migrant labour picking cauliflower crops in East Anglia. The economy has been relatively open to cheap migrant labour, but needs robots because they have all pissed off home. Maybe the robots will up sticks too. Leaving the cauliflowers to rot on the, er, vine.

Some believe robot labour will impact on some humans in quite a negative way: unemployment. Already robots are being developed for everything from construction to surgery to scientific experimentation. Marina Gorbis, head of Californian thinktank The Institute for the Future, reckons the coming decade will see fancy Dan intelligent robots coming for the white-collar jobs that can be automated (like clerical and admin work, and the law) and believes we should concentrate on training our children for only the non-codifiable, non-repetitive, non-routine jobs that require 'higher-level thinking'. Which is, clearly, not many jobs. (Gorbis suggests training kids to make Internet videos or, er, robots. Great.)

A robot-led labour market could leave humans free to fulfil their potential as creative thinkers, inventors, philosophers, artists and artisans. (Which might not be so great: have you met most people?) Or it could leave everyone skint.

But hey, what are you going to do? Smash up the robots like the Lancashire spinners smashed up the Spinning Jenny? We could do that. But that would definitely be asking for some kind of robot uprising. Spinning Jennies could not fight back, not even by spinning. Could the robots? Of course they could. They'd bloody love it.

You're so rubbery, you're so rubbery

Repliee Q2, an uncannily life-like robot developed by roboticists at Osaka University, can mimic such human functions as blinking, breathing and speaking. It also has skin sensors, so can respond to people's touch. And okay, it's not leaping about like Daryl Hannah in *Blade Runner* – it's more sort of wobbling its head and blinking a lot – but still, the days when we thought of wobbling your head and blinking a lot as quintessentially human activities are clearly over.

Repliee Q2's alarmingly realistic face is based on a famous newsreader, Ayako Fujii. So yes, imagine a Japanese Sophie Raworth, in robot form. It's not a big leap. Just to be clear, this 'actroid' was not based on Fujii's features because the Osaka roboticists really fancied her. Not at all. (It was really.)

Robots are getting more lifelike. They are not fooling anyone just yet. But that will come. We are looking at the dawn of the squishybot. Squishybots, the name of which clearly needs some work, are robots constructed from bendy materials, so bringing their appearance closer to organic life-forms. Then there's Frubber, a lightweight elastic polymer that allows realistic movement and has been used to make a robot with the head of Einstein. The name, which clearly needs some work, is a contraction of face and rubber.

Robots with squishy Einstein heads are all good fun. But this push for lifelike robots does, of course, bring up questions of a sexual, sexy nature.

According to futurologist David Levy – author of *Love and Sex with Robots* – the sexbot revolution is on its way. Given the advances, 'love and sex with robots on a grand scale' is not just desirable but inevitable: 'My thesis is this: Robots will be hugely attractive to humans as companions because of their many talents, senses and capabilities.'

By 'talents' he is talking about doing mucky stuff. Robots doing mucky stuff *on a grand scale*. That is the future.

A 2012 report from Victoria University of Wellington, New Zealand, predicts robot red light districts by 2050 and claims this would cut down on sex slavery and also cut down on infections. And what did they call these prostitute robots? They called them 'hoe-bots'. For real.

Meanwhile, a US producer of cutting-edge sex bots, Douglas Hines, has produced Roxxxy, who can do pelvic thrusts and even simulate orgasm. Of course, to some degree, all robot orgasms are simulated. Which would at least remove any uncertainty. 'Were you faking?' 'Yes, I am a robot.'

Roxxxy, who has an enormous tongue, can be programmed with different personalities such as Wild Wendy, S&M Susan, Young Yoko and Frigid Farrah. Quite why anyone who goes to the trouble of getting a sex robot would then want them to play hard to get is a real mystery – but then, human beings are mysterious. Roxxxy also has real human hair – which might be the freakiest bit about it/her.

Do you or do you not fancy the idea of fucking with a robot? This is the sort of question humanity needs to be asking itself.

It won't just stop with sex, of course. Some will prefer to see sexual intercourse with robots as 'making love'. Levy even expects marriage with robots to be legalised by the middle of the century. Would the Church allow such ceremonies to occur in places of worship? (Will there even be places of worship? Yes, there will.)

Even if humans do for some reason decide to just stick with human spouses, there is great potential for a robot bit on the side. Levy believes that while some will see robo-affairs as a form of adultery, some more forgiving spouses will see robo-affairs as essentially meaningless. As long it stays out of sight of the kids, figuratively as well as also literally.

If we are entering a more narcissistic, impatient world of instant gratification – and we are – *of course* you're going to prefer going out with a robot. A robot won't have an hour-long argument about where to go for dinner: robots don't even eat dinner. (Which represents quite a potential saving.) Equally, you can come home at two stinking of booze and pestering your robot for sex, and you won't even be pestering it because it's a robot. It'll be like: 'Yeah, knock yourself out, you pissed twat.'

War robots: what are they good for?

But it's not just sex, it's also death. According to one of the famous Three Laws of Robotics, drawn up by SF pioneer Isaac Asimov as a preparatory guide for decent relations between robot and human: 'A robot must not injure a human being or, through inaction, allow a human being to come to harm.'

But really, that's just boring. Robots that don't kill people? What's the point of that? The whole point of robots is to kill people! Preferably their creators, but if not them, then at least someone else.

In fact, robots that kill are very much on the agenda – the military being one of the key funders in the field (and in such volume that the US Future Combat Systems program was called 'the system that ate the army'). And the war robots blow Asimov's rules somewhat: when the humans are fighting, how should the robots pick sides? Toss a coin?

In all, 56 countries are developing robot military devices, to dispense battlefield death with a clinical excellence lacking in most humans. One recent report suggested 40 per cent of the world's armies will become automated by 2020. The Pentagon is pumping astronomical amounts of money into this stuff, for land, sea and air. The US Navy has already started operating robot helicopters with electronic 'brains' that can recognise small pirate boats through 3D laser imaging. Pirates! In an adventure with flying robots. Now that I would pay money to see. Are you listening, Aardman? I want my cut, though. Not like last time.

Iraq and Afghanistan are/were crawling with unmanned drones and bomb disposal bots (in 2008 there were 22 different types of unmanned equipment, and possibly 12,000 units, at work in Iraq). The people who brought us the Roomba vacuum cleaner are also now providing the Pentagon with a new contract for tiny robots called Throwbots that can be air-dropped onto battlefields and work with each other in deadly tiny robot networks (not sure if they hoover up the mess afterwards). Also imminent is MAARS (Modular Advanced Armed Robotic System), a remote-controlled platform complete with machine gun, grenade launchers and a loudspeaker to point out – presumably unnecessarily – that resistance is futile.

It's not difficult to see the benefits of robot soldiers. Robot soldiers really take the effort out of any war effort. Training men to become killing machines takes time and money – why not just start off with killing machines in the first place? In the words of Gordon Johnson of the Pentagon's Joint Forces Command: 'They don't get hungry. They're not afraid. They don't forget their orders. They don't care if the guy next to them has just been shot. Will they do a better job than humans? Yes.'

They don't go on racist rampages. (He didn't say the last bit.)

The military is also, ironically, a pioneer in the field of robot surgery, the USA developing a mobile field hospital pod that means surgery can be done remotely close to the battlefield, thus cutting down the time before soldiers get treated. (If my research on this is anything to go by – it was watching *MASH* – this will free up the surgeons to perform elaborate practical jokes on the more uptight officers in their regiment.)

So, will wars of the future involve expensive robot armies fighting it out? Or expensive robot armies shooting seven bells of hell out of people who can't afford expensive robot armies? I wonder. (Not really, it will be the second one.) (Well, unless the USA and China line up their bots.)

Already, about a third of US warplanes are robots. The Predator drone debuted in the Balkans and has been used extensively in Iraq and Pakistan. It's a whole new, removed way of doing war. The US-based controllers of missile-firing Predator drones (so-called 'cubicle warriors') might consign people to death in the day, only to clock off at five never having seen a battlefield: 'Hi honey, how was work today?' 'Good actually. We've got a cool new game called "Towelhead 2".' (By the way, the video game metaphor in all this technology is underlined by manufacturers even using video game controllers for some of their systems.)

Not that all are happy to use robot warriors without qualms. In June 2012, extraordinary news emerged of Obama's kill list – names of the al-Qaeda operatives slowly being summarily executed by drones in Yemen on the personal say-so of the president after he has consulted his religious books, his conscience and – by implication – his Maker. A US president agonising over St Thomas Aquinas before sending in the killer robots: it's already happened.

Missile-firing drones might be very clever, but for now they still need to be controlled. Eventually they will fly themselves and fire at will. And robot soldiers will be autonomously tasked with making life and death decisions – it seems inevitable. So much for Asimov. (Although he might be pleased that the Pentagon has paid science fiction writers to dream up sci-fi war stuff for them to then go off and invent.)

Robots at war are a game-changer. P. W. Singer, author of *Wired for War: The Robotics Revolution and Conflict in the 21st Century*, hails a revolution, like the introduction of cannons or nuclear weapons: 'one of the most fundamental changes ever in war'. Because we are changing not just the lethality of war (very much so), but the identity of who fights it. 'Humanity's 5,000 year old monopoly over the fighting of war is over,' he says.

Are robot soldiers going to be bigger bastards than real soldiers? With none of the 'good guys' at risk, will it mean anything goes against the 'bad guys'? With humans not being central, the 'warrior ethos' and rules of war will be up for grabs. And wars will become easier to start . . . And there could be malfunctions – like the automated anti-aircraft system that, at a South African training exercise, started 'firing wildly, spraying high-explosive shells at a rate of 550 a minute, swinging around through 360 degrees like a high-pressure hose', killing nine.

Plus there is – oh yes – the possibility that ultra-powerful fighting machines might decide to take over from the humans. Again. Singer says that. Not me. Not this time.

They're independent, are you?

As granddads and teachers never tire of saying, common sense isn't so common. This is particularly true in robotics (granddads and teachers don't say that). Getting robots to do anything realistically human without the years of 'programming' that go into even basic human decision-making processes is a colossal fag; hundreds of millions of lines of code would create the common sense of a six-year-old. Even roboticists can't be bothered with shit like that.

So scientists are looking at ways for robots to become more autonomous – to do the learning themselves. If robots merely do as they are told, they will always be a bit shit. Yes, it is scary. But they need to learn to think for themselves. It's like bringing up children. You cannot be a helicopter parent for your helicopter robot for ever. At some point they just need to cut loose. Cross roads by themselves. Or, as in the case of Ibn Sina, a male Arabic humanoid robot based in the United Arab Emirates University, run their own Facebook page. (Apparently, for a while, it was still on Myspace, the twat.)

The autonomous robots are in the sewers, but also in the air. The University of Pennsylvania's GRASP robotics lab has unveiled an autonomous 'quadrotor' robot that can fly of its own accord – without even the aid of remote control. Maybe one day it will fly to Jamaica. Would it fly there of its own accord? Yes it would, that is what I have just said; pay attention.

Robots at IBE Berlin evolve their own language by agreeing words between themselves for actions like raising their arms. Meanwhile, the University of Sussex-built Eccerobot is the world's first anthropomimetic robot. Yes, you heard that right: the anthropomimetic robots are here! Anthropomimetic robots mimic the human body, with a skeleton and tendons and joints like ours. The hope is that they will learn intelligence like ours by being physically like us. (Artificial intelligence gets discussed in another chapter; let's just assume for now that robots are going to get 'very clever'.) You can shake hands with Eccerobot, though you might not make real friends as it looks like a freakshow.

There are also robots that ape the learning capabilities of children. Zeno is a robot designed by David Hanson of Hanson Robotics, Texas, to grow up alongside his son (a son who will in no way grow up hating robots). The iCub is a boy-child robot designed by Giulio Sandini of the Italian Institute of Technology, based in Genoa. (Incidentally, this location seems weird: I went to Genoa once and it was a city positively drowning in medieval menace and sleazy gloom. Excellent stuff, but an unlikely home for a robotics institute. Just saying.)

Anyway, iCub is a humanoid robot that learns like a child. It repeats actions until it learns where the boundaries are, learning where it ends and everything else begins, building up knowledge of its surroundings like an infant. They have sent out 20 iCubs around the world, including one to Aberystwyth. (I went there once too.) (There's a funicular.)

According to Giulio Sandini: 'In 20 years' time, we will have a system like the iCub which can learn from me the way I learned from my father. You know, behaving like an apprentice. I don't think it's so far in the future.'

So, teaching our robot children how to live. Is this wise? Could we fuck our robot kids up like we fuck up our real kids? We may not mean to, but we do.

I fear a future in which our robot children reach the stage of suddenly seeing our shortcomings and angrily turn on us, yelling: 'I didn't *ask* to be constructed!'

Before killing us in our beds.

Again.

Becoming a bit robot

Of course, robotics also has its place in the human improvement game, but this does provoke a complex set of emotions. When combinations of robot and human are called 'bionic', it sounds cool. But when they're called 'cyborg', it sounds scary. 'Hi, have you met my cyborg wife?' See?

The process has already begun: the first real cyborg – the fully functioning human-robot hybrid – has already been made. And where did this historic man-machine show itself to the human race? In Reading. (Okay, that's the University of Reading, not just Reading.) And what is the name of this hellish creation? His name is Kevin. And should we fear this Kevin from Reading?

Probably not.

Professor Kevin Warwick had a chip resembling a tiny hairbrush implanted in his arm emitting a radio frequency ID with the aim of becoming the first cyborg. And best of luck to him. He can turn the lights on and off by waving his arm. Girls love that kind of thing.

That is not to trivialise this species-bending break-through. He can also open doors at work. More significantly, as his wife Irena has also had the implant, he has felt, in his own neurons, the signals from his wife's nerves – so raising the possibility of computerised telepathy. It's very intimate apparently. Which is quite sweet.

In the University of Vienna, Oskar Aszmann ampu-tated the hands of two disabled patients and gave them bionic hands instead. This bionic hand picks up the same electronic pulses as would control a real hand. You have to train your brain how to send out the right signals but it soon becomes automatic. This is amazing stuff. You would not want people without hands to go without bionic ones.

More mindbendingly (literally), the US military, as well as pioneering prostheses, is trying to develop Aug Cog chips – Augmented Cognition: chips implanted in the brain that allow the implantee to take in – that is, download to their brain – vast amounts of information in one big GULP (giant upload process). Let's hope it doesn't crash.

This is an area moving apace – the news is increasingly peppered with people getting new limbs that respond to the signals from their minds, or disabled people completing marathons with the aid of robot legs – which does seem to herald immediate benefits for people in need of replacement limbs that behave like normal limbs, and more.

But what are we looking at here? Could we be crossing a line, without even seeing the line or perhaps properly appreciating its existence? After all, it's not that far from elective amputation of disabled hands to elective amputation of perfectly able hands. Prosthetics might be better than real hands so you might get people with functional hands wanting better hands. It is only a matter of time before we find that people are demanding their own robot hand, because it is better than their own hand. One with more functions. I want this cut off and that one put on. You won't do it on the NHS? Then I shall go private. Gonna get me a set of i-hands. (Other brands of hands are available.)

In other words, people with money or power could enhance themselves, forming some sort of tech-assisted super-race. This is not idle speculation, but an active debate amongst our friends the transhumanists and posthumanists. Many of them are just itching to parade around the place with their robot hands and would stick a chip in their noggin in the blink of an enhanced eye.

Incidentally, Kevin of Reading's current project is the Animat, a robot that steers around with the help of a pile of 300,000 rat brain cells that scientists had grown in a lab and which had started working together – working together to steer a robot. Which sounds good, albeit maybe now we need to worry about rats taking over.

On the negative side, Kevin of Reading finds himself driven by unsuppressible thoughts of attacking humans. He tosses and turns all night with it, making the lights go on and off.

Where will it end? Apart from with the robots tearing us limb from limb, obviously?

Could all humanity embrace robots in the way of the elderly Japanese, in their robot pants cuddling their robot seals?

We should certainly beware of the emotional bonds that humans can form with robots (despite an occasional – that is, total – lack of reciprocity). Yasuyuki Toki, a researcher at NEC System Technologies, tells of a talking robot on wheels lent to a family for research. When the robot was taken away for an upgrade, the child cried so much the family refused have anything more to do with robots.

'People aren't going to be able to throw away robots even when they break,' said Toki.

So that's weird. But is it weird? Maybe we in the West are the weird ones. If you can cuddle a stuffed toy and name it, why not a robot?

Will the robots doing all the work strip us of the dignity of labour? Will robots even do all the work, or just some of the work for some of the people? And will we love them? Yes we will. Because we are soppy bastards. Maybe we'll even love the ones spraying leaden death. Already, soldiers in Iraq have braved enemy fire to 'save' wounded bomb disposal bots.

Maybe we'll love the robots too much. And maybe we will even give them rights.

Psychologists are finding that people tend to treat robots as something between an inanimate object and a living machine – not 'alive or dead like an animal, but also not the same as a lawn mower or computer'. But, crucially, the more 'socialised' they become, and the more they look and act 'like us', the greater the respect we accord them. (Though when they seem *too much* like us, we flip over into being freaked out.)

What does this mean in practice? Maybe you'd be okay with kicking a Roomba hoover bot, or locking a robot dog out of the bedroom at night. But, what if I were to run at the Japanese Sophie Raworth, and push her over? Would you be okay with that? Or if I smacked her upside the head with a rolled-up newspaper? Or would that be cruel in some way?

Already a government report piloted by Sir David King, the UK's chief scientific adviser, has mooted a time when robots will need rights – that, as these 'new digital citizens' are putting their 'lives' on the line in wars and stuff, they can reasonably expect to be looked after, including robo-healthcare and benefits (I'm not making this up).

Debate on the ethics of this is all new, with practice running ahead of the debate; after all, we've already built a Graham Norton you can shag without his consent, so it's a tad Wild West out there.

But, worryingly, the International Bar Association has already felt the need to run a mock trial in which a conscious computer battled a corporation that was trying to disconnect it.

Many have prophesied the robot takeover, but few have seen it coming through the courts.

CHAPTER 3: ENERGY

Ambassador, you are despoiling us

Thus far humanity has had the benefit of 2 billion years' worth of accumulated energy just lying around on, or in, the ground, and now we need to develop – and quick – sources of energy that don't clusterfuck the environment or leave us beholden to Vladimir Putin; otherwise the planet will get either a) very hot or b) very dark. Or very hot and very dark. This is in the context of a world that gets 85 per cent of its energy from coal, oil and natural gas.

The politicians don't seem to be feeling the urgency here. At the landmark UN climate change conference in Copenhagen in 2009, world leaders failed to agree a coherent strategy to combat climate change. At the end of the conference, they did not vote on the draft agreement they had bodged up. Instead, they merely 'noted' its existence. They similarly raised their hands to 'note' the quality of the catering, giving the sandwiches the same official international status as the world mission to avert climate chaos, or conspicuous lack of one. The catering really was excellent.

The 2010 Cancun conference offered some progress on the substantive issues, but still no climate agreement (and apparently the lunch wasn't up to much).

However the 2011 Durban conference, in Durban, did

reach an agreement on environmental matters. So that's good. It agreed . . . that there should be an agreement. And who can say they are wrong?

The agreement will be legally binding, which is good. Legally binding: that's the law. But it hasn't actually been made, which is not so good. It might be done by 2015 (to come into effect in 2020). But given that it took 25 years – over two decades since the signing of the Kyoto Protocol – to agree to have an agreement, possibly best not hold your breath. It certainly doesn't bode well that most world leaders didn't even bother turning up for the June 2012 Rio Earth Summit. But hey: these are important people, with a lot of other stuff on their (snack) plates. And it's not like it's a crisis or anything. Oh, no, hang on . . .

There is an ingrained symbolism here. If we cannot keep the lights on, it will be dark and the beasties will get us; this is both the darkness in our souls, and also the darkness wherein you cannot see properly what you are doing. Maintain a non-intermittent power grid or Voldemort, Sauron and the Gremlins all come knocking on the door. Darkness is death, light is life. It's Jesus versus the Gremlins – that's what we're looking at here. Don't feed them after midnight. Don't get them wet. (That's Gremlins, mainly. I don't know if you can feed Jesus after midnight and can get him wet; I'm no theologian.)

So who will save us? Thankfully, underneath the political inaction, or slow action, or backwards action, there is inventing action. Scientists, billionaires, nutters, shysters: all are busily beavering away on sorting everything out for us all. Some are experimenting with turning pond algae into fuel, and developing wood-fired cars. Oh, yes: wood-fired cars. They exist.

Meanwhile, with wind and solar and the other stars of the 'renewable mix', work is going on to find clean sources of energy that don't sound mental to power our natty new electric cars. Oh, yes: electric cars. They exist. Possibly you knew that.

If we can only generate enough clean electricity – and store it in things like hydrogen fuel cells – we'll be golden. (Although the fuel cells also need perfecting, so we'd better get a move on with those too.) Is nuclear fusion the answer to limitless electricity? Still. Yes, scientists are hailing nuclear fusion *again*. Like rock, nuclear fusion became popular in the 1950s and never really went away, albeit it cyclically gets eclipsed by various forms of dance music (that's rock, not fusion). Long live rock!

Or can we, in fact, just magic away the effects of climate change, and thus carry on mindlessly burning fossil fuels? The messianic super-rich are funding their own form of saving the world, so-called geo-engineering, which is actually a competition to come up with the maddest schemes to stop the biosphere collapsing – from massive sunshades in space on down to spraying chemicals into the sky.

Good old the super-rich. They could just be jetting off to their private islands, but instead they are being mad on our behalf.

More energy than you can shake a stick at

I once saw on the news eel-powered Christmas tree lights. And who could not see footage of a tree with lights powered by electric eels floating around nearby and think: 'Well, if we can do that, what *can't* we do? Verily, we are like gods!'?

All we need is enough eels and we shall power the Earth!

And it doesn't stop there; nutters have engaged in all manner of seriously imaginative enterprises to save the world. There are vehicles that run on coffee and vehicles that run on chocolate and vehicles that run on watermelon – vehicles you would actively relish sucking up the fumes from.

The energy nutters see energy everywhere – and, in a strictly physics sense, they are right to. One recently unveiled gas mask-like device – the AIRE – even converts the energy from the air you breathe out into electricity and can be worn as you 'sleep, walk, run, read a book, among other possibilities' (do they mean sex?). Okay, so you are essentially wearing a terrible mask, all the time, to capture a rather negligible amount of energy. But it's still one way of doing your bit. You can literally not waste your breath.

Or your fat. In 2007, a nattily futuristic-looking speedboat called the *Earthrace* went around the world, allegedly powered by human fat. There is no shortage of human fat just yet. Could this be the answer? The vessel was powered by biodiesel derived from human fat taken during liposuction operations from the boat's skipper, a New Zealand biofuels enthusiast and conservationist called Pete Bethune, plus two other (formerly fat) volunteers. This story stretches credulity, of course – unless they were somehow putting on new fat with an on-board supply of Fanta, scotch eggs and Pringles before taking it in turns to continually go under the knife in an impromptu below-deck operating theatre/galley. (Maybe they did do that.)

Anyway, you need not even waste your poo. There is power in poo – and all organic substances – so it's ironically a more palatable idea than many.

A huge new €12m algae plant near Cadiz in Spain is hoping to use the sun to encourage the algae to feed on the poo to produce clean energy – well, perhaps not clean energy, but certainly green energy. Sewage treatment works, power plants and places with lots of livestock (i.e. cow poo) are working on this kind of thing right now. Others are using photosynthesis in actual ponds. Think pond, generally think: stagnant, undynamic, almost wholly crap, energy-wise. But with open pond technology, not any more. Think pond, think energy.

Always up for saving the world in any way he can that doesn't involve not selling monopolistic operating systems that crash all the time, Bill Gates, a new energy maven, is down with algae and has announced his investment in the sector: 'The number of ways to do things with algae is pretty amazing,' he reckons.

Remember: this is the guy who saw there was a future in computers.

Others have mooted putting a fast-growing algae into the sea, to multiply and thus soak up CO_2. This was put on hold when people considered it might get out of hand – a fast-growing algae released into the oceans. I'm no expert, but it does seem to me that a fast-growing algae released into the oceans is exactly the sort of thing that will very obviously go wrong. Four words: 'algae' and 'absolutely fucking everywhere'.

Scientists in North Carolina are working with micro-organisms called extremophiles that live in acidic water. Apparently you leave them in the dark and, without the aid of any other energy source, they suck in carbon dioxide and turn themselves into liquid fuels like butanol. Again, I remain sceptical, if only because they are called extremophiles, which is a very silly name.

And some Americans have managed to make pickups powered by wood – which sounds stupid and probably is. A Pennsylvania group calling itself the Wood Power Energy Corporation is dedicated to making the 'ligneous combustible' (that is, wood) a primary source of fuel. Their pickup runs on wood, and it works. Wood gasification (which is a technical term, but also a good phrase) works by literally vaporising the wood.

So it works. But, crucially: can you scale that up so it serves the engines of the whole planet? Logs? I'm no expert, so I'll admit I just don't know. Could you, though, power all the engines of the world with wood? Could you?

We just don't know.

But no. I'll go with no.

Look, maybe the nutters will see us through; maybe they are not nutters, but visionaries – or at least, visionary nutters. But most of these ideas generally falter on issues like: too expensive; doesn't work; does work, but can't be scaled up; or a tragic combination of these.

That is to say, they all sound great in different ways, but share one common problem: they don't work. Also, watermelons should probably be considered first and foremost a foodstuff for the people, rather than a foodstuff for the people's cars. Still, best of luck to them.

Nutters, eh?

Wind farms kill your kids and have it off with your wife

The scientific consensus claims the basic baseload energies of the future will be solar and to a lesser extent wind, nuclear fission and, if we can perfect it, nuclear fusion. The rest are 'just bollocks' (they don't quite say this – they say they are 'part of the mix' – but that's what they mean). It seems a tad rude to call geothermal, tidal and hydroelectric power bollocks – they are all decent and honourable enough, but can only work in enough places to contribute minority energy – but that's the cold hand of science for you.

The first wind turbine to successfully deliver power to a national grid was installed in Vermont, New England, in 1941, on a hilltop known as Grandpa's Knob. Yes, this historic turbine was called Grandpa's Knob. Let us not make a big thing of that. Anyway, since the erection of Grandpa's Knob (hur hur, I said 'Grandpa's Knob') wind farms have been perpetually about to happen. But the investment has not been there; the antipathy from local residents has.

Today, wind is the power source the right loves to hate – it is variously a 'joke', 'the greatest scam of our age' and a 'bubble'. Prince Philip even called wind energy 'a fairy tale' – although who is *he* to talk about fairy tales? Recent *Daily Mail* headlines have claimed 'Wind turbines can't cope with UK weather . . .', 'Wind farms can actually INCREASE climate change . . .' and 'Wind turbine EXPLODES . . .'. They probably also encourage anti-royalist paedophilia in areas sensitive to house price fluctuation – who can say?

But wind farms out to sea – who could complain about that? Looking out to sea can be a fairly unthrilling experience; a few gently whirring turbines on the horizon is surely a positive boon. And wildlife, like the bats whose signals are sometimes thrown by land-based wind farms, could breathe again. Except for those bats tempted to venture out onto the high seas, but they're just asking for trouble. (People also complain about the number of birds killed by flying into the blades of wind turbines. Two words: 'natural', 'selection'.)

Anyway, it turns out that wind farms at sea are prone to rust and other problems related to standing in (salt) water. Who knew? At one Danish field, all 80 turbines had to be dismantled and repaired after only 18 months. The potential here for a 20-part thriller about this called *The Turbines* is immense.

Solar power is potentially much more significant. Tens of thousands times more energy than humans use falls from the sun onto the Earth every day; it's practically infinite. Yet solar currently supplies less than half a per cent of the world's energy – though it has a bright future (no pun intended) and an illustrious past (no pun intended there either.)

Leonardo da Vinci proposed building a four-mile wide mirror that could be employed commercially as a source of heat. At the start of the nineteenth century, Napoleon Bonaparte's armies roasted chickens in Egypt using primitive solar boxes. ('Not tonight Josephine, for I am eating chicken that has been cooked in a sun box.') So the idea isn't new; it's obvious.

These days, the Mongolians are leading the charge globally, this time not in charging across Europe on steeds, slaughtering all who resist, but in laying down very many solar panels. Just north of the Great Wall of China, in Inner Mongolia, plans are afoot (funded by China who are bang into solar) to create 2 billion watts of power by laying down 27 million thin-film photovoltaic (PV) solar panels across the Gobi Desert. If successful, and the project has hit many bumps along the way, it could be the first of many deserts to take advantage of all that sun for which deserts are famed. And the lack of other productive stuff to do in deserts (see mirages/crawl on hands and knees/pant).

Apparently, covering Wales in solar panels would satisfy all the Sahara's energy needs. No, that's not right. It's an area of solar panels the size of Wales in the Sahara could provide all the UK's energy needs. Don't worry, no one is planning on covering Wales in solar panels. It wouldn't be worth the hassle.

There are two main forms of solar tech in the race to dominate the putative solar revolution. PV technology takes advantage of how when a light particle hits metal it kicks out an electron to create a current. Pow! Energy! Try it yourself at home. It won't work, but you can try.

Or there is concentrated solar power (CSP), which uses giant mirrors to concentrate heat onto a liquid – oil or water – which makes steam to generate electricity. You can definitely make this work at home – perhaps for the purpose of killing some ants. Zap! Energy! Ant-killing energy!

There are lots of Silicon Valley billionaires toying with solar. Google are siding with PV, ploughing secret amounts of money (but probably not, like, fifty quid) into Nanosolar, a project that employs nanotechnology (more of which later . . . it means 'small technology') to hopefully produce low-cost thin-film panels. 'Nanosolar solar cells – cheaper than milk' is one claim they make (like you are ever going to have to choose between the two).

The cool and groovy Silicon Valley types are worried about governments' seeming paralysis over energy and believe we – that is, they – should start putting in place other plans. They believe they are proven at spotting winners, and want to turn saving the planet into a sort of *Dragons' Den* scenario. And who are we to stand in their way? After all, they are very knowledgeable about search engines and skateboards, er . . .

Even with current technology (which is expensive and inefficient), the International Energy Agency believes solar could produce a quarter of the world's energy by 2050. But with innovations like cheapo and more efficient nano-cells, any surface can capture the sun's energy, so it's game on.

One thin material resembling denim could even coat the outsides of buildings, meaning even town planners will one day have to wrestle with the eternal question: 'How much denim is too much denim?'

After denim buildings, we might even see denim clothes (maybe you find that easier to imagine than denim buildings). In 2011, US designer Andrew Schneider launched his limited edition solar-powered bikini, a slinky two-piece capable of charging a smart-phone or MP3 player as the wearer soaks up some rays. So that's the solar-powered bikini. Can the solar-powered mankini be far behind?

Bill Gates is not down with solar-powered mankinis – or solar power generally. He has noticed 'a mind-blowing' problem with solar. 'People deeply underestimate what a huge problem this day-night issue is if you're trying to design an energy system involving solar technology that's more than just a hobby,' he reckons.

What Gates is saying here is: yeah Google, whatever, fucking wasters, haven't you even, like, noticed the sun goes down yet? Get a load of my algae!

We have ignition! (or at least we expect to have ignition within a few decades, given adequate funding and other certain provisos)

Does nuclear fusion (the futuristic, safer version of nuclear) offer limitless energy supplies around the corner, or are the scientists just having a laugh?

Fusion is a tricky and elusive mistress. Sébastien Balibar, of the French National Centre for Scientific Research, came over all Eric Cantona when he put it like this: 'We say that we will put the sun into a box. The idea is pretty. The problem is, we don't know how to make the box.'

Yes, or how to put the sun in it. (Nice one, Sébastien.)

Fusion differs from fission – the method of current nuclear power stations – by fusing together atoms rather than smashing them apart. This sounds nicer and it is nicer: fusion produces no waste and in the worst case scenario of a meltdown or accident, the reaction simply stops rather than blowing the whole place to Kingdom Fuck and spreading deadly radiation all over the shop à la Chernobyl and Fukushima. Fusion promises nothing less than exceedingly cheap energy with exceedingly few downsides. Which is a good balance.

Sadly, though, it doesn't work. As sceptics never tire of pointing out, fusion is always 50 years away. But as supporters hit back: without funding, it will not be 50 years away – it will be never. And anyway, these days it's allegedly more like 20 or 30 years away, which does actually roll by surprisingly quickly.

Actually, it is not quite correct that fusion doesn't work. Fusion is regularly achieved – with increasingly good results. It just doesn't work without using up as much energy as it produces. Energy plants that use up as much energy as they produce are really not doing a great job, energy production-wise. To make a fusion plant economic, each fusion event would need to be around 40 times more effective. Nearly there! Kind of.

Is it like putting the sun in a box or putting the sun in a bottle, though? The approach of the UK's biggest fusion facility, the Culham Centre for Fusion Energy in Oxfordshire, involves making a gas so hot that the electrons are stripped away from the atomic nuclei to form an intriguing subatomic soup called plasma. You can literally bottle that (in an 'intense magnetic bottle', of all things) to produce clean, abundant energy and a side order of helium – which is useful for making funny high voices.

A rival project at the US National Ignition Facility (cool name) is working on using a very powerful laser to cause fusion in tiny bits of deuterium and tritium. Unfortunately, the laser itself uses titanic amounts of energy, which is not so good. Still, they call this process 'igniting a star with laser light' – which does sound pretty cool. Who wouldn't want to ignite stars with laser lights?

'We've done fusion at fairly high levels already,' said NIF director Dr Ed Moses. 'Even on Sunday night, we did the highest fusion yield that has ever been done.' (Even Sunday nights are big nights in Fusion Town.)

Dr Ed Moses is a good name. And fusion is clearly a good idea. It has remained a good idea all this long while that people have been talking about and trying to perfect it. But we'd best not rely on it to save the planet in the short term, given that it doesn't work.

Fission is not 50 years away. Fission is now. Fission works – it powers whole nations, like France. There are quite well-publicised downsides here too, though (not least what to do with the waste and the paucity of long-term uranium supplies). But can these downsides be overcome? This is something the green movement has been stabbing itself in the eye about of late. 'But we need nuclear to avoid climate change.' 'You are a bastard.' 'Diiiiiiiiiiie!' 'Banzai!!!!' That kind of thing.

Bill Gates is down with fission, but better fission, fission that is child-friendly – or at least unlikely to give rise to children with two heads. He is investing in a group called Intellectual Ventures who sound like they might sit around discussing Heidegger ('I feel emptiness, ja?'), but are actually trying to invent better nuclear power stations (essentially: more power, less waste). 'We've got a new nuclear design, a generation four,' Gates said. 'On paper it's quite amazing. And when I say on paper, I really mean in a supercomputer where we simulate everything.'

That's right: they use computers now. They are so beyond designing nuclear reactors on paper.

By the way, it should be pointed out that you shouldn't try splitting the atom at home.

When in 2011 a 31-year-old Swedish man Richard Handl was found to have attempted to split the atom in his kitchen, with a stash of uranium, radium (scavenged from clock hands) and americium, he was rightly halted by the authorities and arrested. Handl later admitted his efforts were 'crazy'. He was, he claimed, just 'curious'.

Handl is apparently one of an international community of 'amateur nuclear scientists' – a phrase which should not exist. Not even a little bit.

Sometimes the craziest ideas are actually the sanest . . . (and sometimes they are not)

There may be an alternative to alternative energy sources. Because, you know, we could just stick our fingers up our arses and hope that geo-engineering pans out. That is: someone literally flicks a switch and all the climate chaos problems evaporate; the sun's heat gets reflected back whence it came and the pollution is sucked up by wonderful new sucky things.

Yes it's insanely dangerous, intervening wildly in the complex natural environment, but sometimes doing the insanely dangerous thing is doing the right thing. Isn't that how it works? At least sometimes? Actual ideas posited as serious geo-engineering solutions here include putting huge mirrors in space that reflect the sunshine away from Earth. Just reflect it into space! Simple! One fantastic idea, again in Mongolia, involves cooling down Ulan Bator with a massive ice-cube (river ice that has been artificially thickened through the winter months). This poses great dangers – not least that the whole city's population might be tempted to touch it with their tongues.

Bill Gates, perhaps inevitably – God, he's driven – has been funding various schemes to geo-engineer the atmosphere. His favourite involves seawater-spraying machines that spray up water to create more clouds to keep the sun's heat away from Earth. (Remember: this is a guy who saw there was a future in algae.)

This plan would require a great deal of energy upfront – an estimated 1,900 ships might be needed to keep Earth's temperature from rising. Plus, it would be cloudy. But we need a Plan B! And that 'B' does not – repeat *not* – stand for Bollocks.

Gates also funded plans to make clouds whiter by spraying them with particles of sulphur so they reflect more heat back up. Just how do you get the sulphur up there? Through a massive hose held aloft by blimps the size of Wembley Stadium tethered 14 miles above the Earth.

Okay, so the scientists involved – including Harvard's Professor David Keith – are not sure this idea will work, but so what? One researcher, Hugh Hunt, said: 'The nice thing about it is that we can really have a knob, if you like, which we can control to adjust the rate at which we inject these particles.'

It's okay! We can have a knob! They will actually be able to control the rate at which they fuck up the atmosphere. Everything's under control!

Unfortunately, climatologists have expressed fears that such schemes could easily lead to massive disturbances in the global weather system, leading to huge crop failures, leading to mass starvation and death for millions. Such untold misery would at least provide plenty of work for the Bill Gates Foundation.

Also well into this madpants shit are the co-founder of Skype and Kazaa, Niklas Zennström (whose Zennström Philanthropies has funded geo-engineering research) and tar sands magnate Murray Edwards (who reportedly owns a major stake in Carbon Engineering, whose wasteful carbon capturing schemes have been ridiculed in the *Washington Post* for potentially depriving 53 million people of water, by using up all their water). Oh, and Richard Branson.

In 2011, Richard Branson helped fund the Royal Society's inquiry into deflecting sunlight back from whence it came through his Carbon War Room charity which seeks to 'harness the power of entrepreneurs to unlock market-driven solutions to climate change'. The walls of his actual 'War Room' – which exists (it's in Washington, DC) – are adorned with inspirational quotes from the likes of Winston Churchill and Albert Einstein. And Richard Branson. 'All hail me! Richard Branson!' Stuff like that.

Of course, billionaires might be biased here: particularly against anything that tends towards people spending less money. There is profit in people spending their money – that is basic economics (very basic economics). Indeed, Branson revealed in 2009 that this so-called Plan B option would actually be his preferred Plan A: 'If we could come up with a geo-engineering answer to this problem, then

Copenhagen wouldn't be necessary. We could carry on flying our planes and driving our cars.' Virgin planes, preferably.

So humans are fucking up the atmosphere, but if we fuck it up back again we can hopefully de-fuck the situation almost completely, so enabling the continuing fucking and de-fucking of the atmosphere without care or concern. We are cleared for take-off!

Some bright sparks have even suggested we genetically engineer our way out of trouble – by engineering plants that are particularly thirsty for CO_2. Or by engineering a breed of tiny vegetarians. In a 2012 paper called 'Human Engineering and Climate Change', one S. Matthew Liao of New York University proposed a new breed of GM humans with less energy intensive diets. Scientists could breed a mild aversion to eating meat, or select genetically towards having smaller children. (Yes, this is essentially screening out the big kids.) We could even, he reckons, programme in more empathy and altruism, perhaps by introducing the hormone oxytocin, to breed humans who more naturally feel inclined to act towards the common good. 'Kids these days! Always acting towards the common good!'

Liao argues that this bio-engineering is less risky, in the grand scheme of things, than geo-engineering. And maybe it is (many things are). But that does not make it right. Also, a community of teeny little do-good vegetarians bleating on about caring for others: for those who have not undergone this dramatic transformation, the impulse to beat them up would be too great. (Don't get me wrong: I am strongly anti-bullying.) (But they would sort of be asking for it.)

Of all the big 'ifs' discussed here, geo-engineering is quite clearly the iffiest. Many have expressed concerns about this narrow, filthy-rich clique lobbying governments and closing down others' options. Even Professor Keith of the sulphur-spraying blimps has admitted: 'Concerns that a small group [is] dominating the debate are legitimate.' Indeed, Prof.

And whatever did happen to Plan A? The whole less carbon, more green energy strategy – you know, the one that might actually work. Humans are pretty ingenious. Shouldn't we be making some headway with that? A recent study co-authored by one Stanford and one UC-Davis academic calculated that, using today's technology, the world could be reliant on sustainable energy in 20-40 years – albeit with an effort 'comparable to the Apollo moon project or constructing the highway system'.

Probably the study is exaggerated and utopian, but that doesn't make the general idea – of doing stuff – wrong. On the one hand we have the possibility of climate chaos, displaced populations, conflict over resources – and last ditch maverick interventions in ecologies with unpredictable results; on the other, technologies that, if we put the time and money into developing them, could provide energy for all for ever.

Anyway, it seems like it should rank higher on human to do lists than dithering over snacks. Or letting things fuck up so badly that it seems like a good idea to let Branson have a go.

CHAPTER 4: THE INTERNET

World wide web

Researchers at New Zealand's Human Interface Technology Laboratory have used a Microsoft Kinect to augment reality, showing imaginary spiders crawling around the room – supposedly to help sufferers of arachnophobia in what they call 'virtual reality exposure treatment'. That's good: having imaginary spiders crawling over your desk, up the walls, up your arm . . . this sounds like a brilliant way to overcome any traumatic feelings you may have about arachnids – and, indeed, reality generally. Are the spiders really there? Aaaaargh. That is what the arachnophobes would think, and perhaps even say out loud.

This is the future of the Internet: spiders. Well, not spiders especially, but augmenting net stuff onto real stuff, plus beaming the Internet directly into your eyes with Internet contact lenses. For, while on one level the Internet has already happened – the Internet: yes, I've seen that. This is what you probably think – the Internet has a far greater capacity to mess with your mind than it already has thus far. What if the Internet has barely begun? What if, in the words of economist John Steele Gordon (great name), 'We are now at the point with the Internet that they were with the railroad in 1850. It's just the beginning.'?

In terms of its utility for mankind, the net is up there with clocks and ploughs (and you can't watch old clips of Lovejoy on a plough) (not yet, anyway). But can we handle what this new-fangled Internet's going to bring our way? Will things fall apart, the centre not holding, because of the Internet? Will it even threaten our family bonds? A recent ideal home exhibition in the USA displayed a house with separate entrances for each member of the family – so each member can reach their room and start surfing without having to talk to one another. There was even an option for separate kitchen and bathroom facilities. 'Who left the seat up? Oh, that would have been me.'

Already, our notions of 'shopping' – and therefore 'towns' – have been radically altered. Tesco recently showcased online avatars to show how we would appear in their clothes (in Tesco clothes, we will always look awful), to save you the trouble of going and trying them on. Mind you, if we are never going out, even down to the shops, then what is the point of new clothes? Have you even thought of that, Tesco, you arseholes?

We are changing, clearly – but are we changing up or down? Are we, in short, turning ourselves into doltish lovers of froth who cannot retain information and therefore ultimately wisdom? One UCLA study suggested that continual flitting about looking at five things at once stopped the brain from attaining the concentration levels needed for really understanding complex matters. A growing band of academics fear that the rise of social networking is creating an army of self-centred, attention deficit, 'infantilised' young people, forever craving novelty. (They don't use words like 'tossers', but that's what they mean.)

Of course, Plato once complained about the new technology of 'writing' and how that would damage memory skills, so maybe all change causes these kinds of debates (and Plato did write some fairly major books – so he wasn't really walking it like he talked it).

And if Google knows more about us than we know about ourselves, what does that mean for individual identity? Already people have concerns about privacy, what with Google spying on them constantly and even rebranding the planet.

Anyway, the Internet, far from proving a fad, is destined to be embedded in all things – cars, toasters, clothes . . . It's going to beamed into our eyes and onto wallscreens in our homes . . . Safe to say the future will not be a good place for people who don't like the Internet.

More real than real

Currently, society is still learning to negotiate Web 2.0, the so-called social web. But already emerging is Web 3.0, the convergence of the virtual and physical world – what has been dubbed the Metaverse.

This is already happening in ad campaigns and apps, with information being overlaid onto the world before us through a mobile device in a delicate – well, often quite clunky – marriage of the net and reality (reality being the old fashioned 'world' you download with your 'eyes').

This 'augmented reality' (AR) can reveal the history of nearby buildings, whether that hotel close by has any rooms free, who painted that picture, whether people rate that café, and show where tube lines are running under your feet. Ultimately, it will provide information on who you are talking to. The potential for arseholes to come up with hellish new chat-up lines here is immense.

As might perhaps be expected, Google is bang up for augmenting reality. Co-founder Sergey Brin is reportedly deeply involved in the development of Google's AR headset Project Glass – or, in the popular, much better parlance, 'Google Goggles' – currently being fine-tuned at the company's secret 'out there' facility, Google X. The super-secret hush-hush Google X facility is thought to be located around the Bay Area. One Google engineer familiar with Google X was quoted in the *New York Times* saying it was run as mysteriously as the CIA — with two offices, 'a nondescript one for logistics, on the company's Mountain View campus, and one for robots, in a secret location'. One for robots?

Prototype Google Goggles have recently been unveiled, placing a little screen above the wearer's right eye, so you can 'read' reality like the short-sighted use bifocals. In the stylish publicity pics, the handsome models do their best to not look like twats from the future. These shots make you think: 'No one's going to wear Internet glasses!' Then again, the same may have been said for all kinds of Internet activities that people went for quite spectacularly. ('Hey, what's the harm? We're *already* twats from the future!')

Apart from the usual tube-line stuff, this project promises much more, including a program to recognise different plants and leaves, so aiding 'curious people, those wishing to avoid toxic plants, and botanists and environmentalists searching for rare plants' (also good for if we start having to forage for food).

It's early days: when demonstrated using a Union Jack on a BBC programme, the goggles failed to identify the flag, thus overlaying nothing over something most schoolkids the world over could name. Nevertheless, according to former Google chief exec – and Silicon Valley colossus – Eric Schmidt: 'This is the beginning of the real revolution in information. You need never be lonely, you need never be bored.' (You'll never leave, he almost added.)

The military are exploring AR too: future soldiers will not augment reality by holding up their smart-phones (that would be stupid), but will have an Internet headset. The pioneering Land Warrior system was tried out by the 9th Infantry in Iraq overlaying with GPS tracking systems, showing the battlefield and the location of allies and enemies, to provide real-life Terminator vision. The system promised to 'enhance the soldier's lethality, survivability, mobility, situational awareness and sustainability.' (Sustainability? What did it do – point out the nearest recycling point?)

The Land Warrior was put on ice as the benefits – all the lethality and so on – were outweighed by the disadvantage of having a fucking computer on your head. A new version is on the way.

So that's Web 3.0. What's next – Web 4.0? Yes. According to futurist John Smart, Web 4.0 will be the semantic web – the Internet properly 'understanding' language and then talking to you.

Tim Berners-Lee, the 'Father of the Internet' who developed the Internet Esperanto of HTML in 1990, is still hard at work on developing this more 'intelligent' web which will see the Internet attempting to understand its own content – and offering up search results with some lateral 'thinking'. Searches would make conceptual links, fishing out relevant people or books, and could be personally tailored to your interests and likes/dislikes built up over time. Internet searches are currently fairly useful, but not compared to what's coming.

Google is also into the semantic web: yes, it doesn't just want to help mediate your experience of reality, it also wants an Internet that understands what you want more than you do. According to Eric Schmidt, the whole idea of 'searching' – as in typing in words – should just go hang itself: 'Perhaps a decade from now, you will think, well, that was interesting, I used to type, but now it just knows.'

They are proposing, for you, nothing less than a personal Internet layer. 'How does it know? Well, on mobiles we know where you are, down to the nearest foot. You've chosen to log in, with your permission, and it knows where you are and it can provide a personalised service.'

Schmidt always says 'with your permission' because otherwise people get scared and cross; but there's nothing sinister here. This is Google we're talking about. How could it be sinister?

What might come after Web 4.0, though? Web 5.0? That does seem to be the direction things are headed in.

By the way, Sergey Brin's business card is said to be simply a piece of silvery metal decorated with the letter 'X' . . . which is not very helpful. Is he not on e-mail? And does he actually think this is cool?

More internet than you could shake a stick at

Pretty soon, touch-screen tech will look old fashioned: touch-air technology is on its way.

Hackers are apparently jumping all over Kinect like rabid dogs: students at MIT are using the gaming technology (it's a sensor that reacts to movements and words) to track all ten digits of your hand. We are but moments from communing with computers by waving our hands in the air. This is one instance when everyone must by law say the words: 'Minority Report'. The others are if you encounter any hints of adverts addressing you personally or if you come across Samantha Morton in a bath. (She is very fond of baths. And why not?)

So you will have the Internet at – even *in* your fingertips. And you will have the Internet in your eyes. Pretty soon, AR headsets and glasses will seem old-fashioned. At a laboratory at Seattle's University of Washington, Babak Parvis is developing a contact lens to use microlasers to send an image directly onto the retina – the information beamed straight through your eye, overlaid onto standard reality. Users could instantly check their health status, or GPS, or messages, or watch films, or get spammed, and they wouldn't even need to turn their head because it would be in their eyes. (Incidentally, this smart contact lens would be a wireless device – users would not have wires coming out of their eyes.)

This is not so far from augmenting your brain with the Internet – using implants to break down the divide between your brain and all things all together. So the Internet in your brain, and the Internet also in all things. People are seriously talking about an 'Internet of things' – the Internet in all things everywhere all the time. *Everything* will be connected: fridges, forests (recording rainfall, etc.), even your toaster. . . .

Vint Cerf is another Father of the Internet who is now employed by Google as 'Chief Internet Evangelist'. He is quite keen on the Internet. He posits a world where you talk to your fridge: 'It won't seem strange to interact with the refrigerator, even remotely,' he said.

He is actively excited about talking to his fridge. An information-age fridge. What will that do? It will keep things cool, essentially, but it will also do so much more. If you are worried about your milk while out and about, you can ask your fridge about it. And your fridge will tell you.

Your clever fridge might even suggest recipes based on the contents: Beer and Mouldy Broccoli Surprise, perhaps. Or Leftovers.

And your toaster will be wired too. Wildly old-fashioned people think toasters are just there to make toast. But old toast is square. Check out toast 3.0; it's in the round. In the future, burnt toast will be the Internet's fault.

Meanwhile, in the supermarket (will there even be supermarkets? Yes there will), products might contact your fridge – or vice versa – about goods that are running low. Sauce bottles might attempt to engage you in conversation as you pass by. ('Oi, mate. Sauce? You need some sauce. Mate . . . Sauce . . . Mate . . . Fucker's ignoring me.' That kind of thing).

There will be an Internet of things in another way too – with objects contributing to the Internet itself. Perhaps even, it has been suggested, blogging (I'm not making that up).

So the Internet – free-flowing information – will be all around. According to Yale computer scientist David

Gelernter, you might have 'a scooped-out hole in the beach where information from the cybersphere wells up like seawater'. Imagine getting paid to say things like this. Good on him, I say.

What could this possibly mean, though? We first need to appreciate that the Internet is, in the view of some, 'alive' and could actually be heading towards some kind of consciousness of its own. According to 'digital prophet' Kevin Kelly, another deep tech thinker and Silicon Valley legend, the Internet is a 'magic window' that provides a 'spookily godlike' perspective on existence. 'I doubt angels have a better view of humanity,' he writes. (The Internet: better than angels.)

'Look at what is coming: technology is stitching together all the minds of the living, wrapping the planet in a vibrating cloak of electronic nerves, entire continents of machines conversing with one another, the whole aggregation watching itself through a million cameras posted daily. How can this not stir all that is organic in us that is sensitive to something larger than ourselves?

'We can see more of God in a cell phone than in a tree frog.'

Yes, he is still talking about the Internet. But he is also talking about God. And he is also talking about vibrating cloaks. (Vibrating cloaks? The best sort of cloaks.) Maybe the Internet is already a god, a really dirty god purveying far more in the way of cumshots than is standard in most of the world's major religions.

So spurting out of the hole in the sand is not just train times, it is the code of existence itself. (Although yes, it could also be train times.)

When you search the internet, does the internet not also search you?

Over the years, Facebook's Mark Zuckerberg has had to apologise for many things. In 2006, he apologised when users expressed anger about the site being visible to non-users. 'Calm down. Breathe. We hear you,' he said, somewhat dickishly.

In 2007, he was forced to apologise for Beacon, a feature that fed users' activities on other sites back to Facebook. 'We simply did a bad job with this release, and I apologise,' he said.

And it's not just Zuckerberg. In 2010, Google had to apologise when their social networking site Google Buzz streamed through to its message service G-Mail to reveal followers' e-mails. That same year, Google had to make numerous apologies for all the sensitive data collected on Street View. Although naughty old Eric Schmidt did first fan the flames, saying people who didn't like the invasion could 'just move'. (He later said this was a joke.)

Again in 2010, the EU called Facebook's default privacy settings 'unacceptable' after users found they were giving away everything about themselves, by default. Then in 2012, British and French data protection bodies lambasted Google for its 'vague' privacy policy that failed to specify to users how their personal information would be shared throughout the company's different services.

Being apologised to by billionaires in sweatshirts who are using your private life to make more cash than you can possibly imagine: is this the future of humanity right here?

With all this invading of our privacy, it's certainly almost like they're hell-bent on invading our privacy or something.

Facebook uses its users' 'likes' to laser-focus their ads. Google checks for keywords in the content of e-mails sent through Gmail to better target users. And what's so wrong with that? Have you got a problem with being advertised to on the basis of your computer messages being read? When challenged about such data mining, Schmidt said: 'Google doesn't do data mining.' (He might have been joking again . . . it's hard to tell.)

Data mining is basically following you, following what you do, following how you use your phone, following how you spend your money. But this following is not like stalking. That would be awful. This following is purely for marketing purposes, using this information so they and their advertisers can target you more effectively. Come on, who wants to be shown loads of inappropriate ads?

In a way, you do have to feel these net giants' pain. We show them all this 'us', and then somehow vaguely expect them to not use this 'us-ness' for monetary gain. Actually, maybe we don't even expect that any more. On the other hand, this 'data' being mined here is not so much mere 'data' as 'you'. It is 'you' mining. Digging up all the stuff you do. And recording it *for ever*.

'Mining', the word, even suggests something subter-ranean and dirty. The other word used – harvesting, as in harvesting data – might initially seem nicer, but only goes to show that, where it doesn't directly relate to harvesting crops (the harvest, Harvest Festival etc.), the word harvest tends to have dark connotations: harvesting data, harvesting organs, harvesting the whirlwind . . .

Anyway, unelected, unaccountable companies, well known for their self-deluded and messianic views of themselves, will know absolutely everything there is to know about you. They will know more about you than you will know about yourself, as you will have forgotten because your memory will be shot to fuck because you're always on the Internet. (And the opportunities will only increase as we move into cloud computing – using the Internet as computer memory rather than storing info in actual devices.)

But isn't the Internet a bastion of freedom? Many claims have been made for the Internet bringing down dictators. You know the basic Wikileaks-lovers' line: before social media, people in Cairo could never have known to meet at the big bloody square where all the protesting had been taking place all week. Arranging protests was just impossible – some guys would be by the big clock by the statue in town, others by the industrial estate round by the superstore. It just wasn't worth it.

But the Internet everywhere does sound slightly like never quite escaping the Internet – or those in charge of the Internet (and, in the case of private companies like Facebook, never escaping those in charge of those in charge of the Internet . . . like banks and investment funds). Already, companies spying on people's habits and states spying on people who step outside of normal behaviour have achieved near-total correspondence.

The British government isn't even bothering with secrecy – proposing a law to let it snoop on everyone's e-mails (so GCHQ will be first in the queue for all the good stuff on Gumtree). Meanwhile, the USA's National Security Agency has a budget twice that of the CIA; its Echelon program monitors and data mines virtually all electronic communication in the world. As with the marketeers, they are tracking people in three ways: by their demographic characteristics, age, gender and so on; by psychographics (what they feel and say about things); and behavioural analysis (tracking what they are doing and so predicting what they are likely to do).

The NSA is, in the main, looking for terrorists. But would this data not be gold-dust to advertisers? What a waste! (Not that they would necessarily be marketing to terrorists . . . 'Hey, check out this cool bag of lime . . .')

China is also keen on picking up terrorists – or what we might also call 'bloggers whose views differ from the Party'. Designed by US giants like IBM and General Electric, the Party's 'Golden Shield' project is hoping to use the latest people-tracking technology to instantly identify all inhabitants and track potential trouble-makers.

In 2011, Cisco Systems was sued by Chinese political prisoners for allegedly aiding their imprisonment. In a leaked internal Cisco presentation from 2002, the company suggested its products could address China's goals of 'maintaining stability', 'stop network-related crimes' and 'combat "Falun Gong", evil religion and other hostiles'. (Imprisoned members of the Falun Gong cult were, of course, routinely executed with their organs then being donated to Party officials.) (For implantation that is; they didn't eat them.) (I don't think so, anyway.)

As the prisoners' lawyer Daniel Ward claimed: '(Cisco) aren't just selling routers to a corrupt regime. They are selling the technology, training and software specifically designed to monitor, censor and suppress the Chinese people.' (At the time of writing, the company has vowed to 'vigorously defend' itself against the claims.)

So, yeah: the demo's in the big square where all the shouting people are and – ah, stop hitting me.

Oh what a glorious thing to be: a healthy, grown-up, busy, busy bee

It is well known that H. G. Wells and Pete Townshend out of The Who invented the Internet. (Not together. Separately.)

Townshend invented the Internet for his aborted rock opera project *Lifehouse* in which pollution forces a future population indoors; everyone is connected to each other and fed a constant stream of entertainment through a computerised 'Grid'. Rock'n'roll is dead, only to eventually be revived by rebels who break free from all the IT to get in touch with their inner primitives by putting on rock concerts in the woods (yes, *Lifehouse* would have been quite shit).

Wells first crystallised his more positive vision of the World Brain in his 1921 book *The Salvaging of Civilisation*. This Internet was a global network that gathered all possible human knowledge for improving society and eliminating poverty and war, and spreading beauty. And you could also post footage of your ex-girlfriend in the buff to get back at her for dumping you because she reckons you were getting on to her even though you, like, weren't. (H. G. Wells hated being dumped.)

So from the start, the net could be a utopia or a dystopia. So are we evolving? Or devolving? Or just revolving? Certainly, anyone still capable of any individual thought can tell major changes have already occurred. Some people are taking to this new world of non-privacy with real relish. Too much relish. Here is my world. Welcome. Look over there. There's my pants.

It is now fairly easy to imagine society shifting towards a collective hive-mind – like bees, only not working together to make honey so much as bickering and calling each other's honey 'a fucking shit waste of time LOSER'.

Hey, perhaps the endless debate and discourse of the online world is, in fact, the very essence of Platonic dialogue . . . sorting out ideas, putting down crap ones, working through contradictions. You know, maybe.

But will we be losing more than we gain? In 2010, virtual reality pioneer Jaron Lanier produced a screed called You Are Not a Gadget, in which the geeky worm turned, or at least questioned. On the new so-called wisdom of crowds, he has said: 'If you ask a crowd to do something creative or constructive, you end up with a dull average . . . The types of artists we get this way have a predictable, likable, non-controversial quality. I don't think we'll get a Kurt Cobain or a Clash through this.' Because Jaron Lanier is pretty punk rock (that's what he's saying here).

Of course, in 1977 The Clash were loudly railing against everybody sitting round watching television – and yes, that *was* the 1970s, largely: kids watching telly all Saturday morning; blokes watching *World of Sport* all Saturday afternoon. A lot of set was going down. *Are You Being Served?* That was on a *lot*. I digress . . .

Anyway, Lanier wonders if we are surrendering too much of our humanity to technology. Are we? And are we also surrendering our brains? People younger and younger are integrating more and more constant technology into their lives, spending more and more time online (even infants) (even foetuses) (not foetuses) (although, in a way – yes, foetuses: think about it). By some estimates, children as young as five spend an average of six hours a day in front of some kind of screen, and teenagers and adults even more. (In 2010, in the USA, it was estimated that 8-18-year-olds' daily goggle-time was eleven hours.) (Which barely seems possible.)

The research in this area is still very slight, but something is happening: one small 2012 study in China suggested the brains of teens who used the Internet were different to the brains of non-users. The brain is dynamic and malleable, and this and other studies suggest that net use is changing the contacts inside our heads and affecting how we remember and concentrate.

In fact, we don't bother remembering – it's all on the net anyway. Computers do make much dull rote learning (or so-called 'school') unnecessary – but how can you have coherent, critical opinions if you don't know *anything*? One recent study by Columbia professor Betsy Sparrow found that when net-users are asked questions they cannot immediately answer, instead of thinking about the question, they think about a computer – that is, *where* they could get the answer. When asked 'Are there any countries with only one color in their flag?', the participants think not about flags, but about computers. The report concluded: 'We are becoming symbiotic with our computer tools.'

When asked questions about flags, we should think about flags. Otherwise something has definitely been lost. This is less using our computer as tools and more as crutches – mental crutches, with powerpacks and leads and shit. We are using mental crutches and we have not even broken our brains! What has become of us?

More worryingly than losing all sense of general knowledge, there are even fears that constant net/computer use also erodes our capacity for empathy. Yes: some people argue that all those shooting games, slagging people off anonymously and wanking might be affecting people's ability to interact with other people. It may even be that the sheer amount of information we now have to process stunts our capacity for empathy. Perhaps we need shooting games that show the victims' families? Or to invent a game called 'International Criminal Court'? You know, just thinking out of the box here.

Maybe it doesn't matter and we should just go with the flow. Maybe we can be just as happy and fulfilled having shed our old ways and thrown in our lot as part of some collective hive of flighty gossips, never alone, never bored, always knowing the time of the next train.

Or maybe the Internet is like the telly: really good, but you have to turn it off from time to time.

CHAPTER 5: NANOTECHNOLOGY

I believe in miracle materials

The strongest material known to man has been discovered by two Russian men in Manchester using sticky tape and pencils. Now, that sounds made up, but it isn't.

This new wonder stuff, graphene, was discovered by two Russian expat scientists based at Manchester University and is held forth as one of the first major miracles of nanotechnology – the science of the manipulating of stuff at utterly minuscule, in fact downright atomic levels.

Konstantin Novoselov and Andre Geim received the Nobel Prize for Physics in 2010 for discovering graphene, a one-atom thick chicken wire-like lattice of carbon, using Scotch Tape and a pencil (or a few pencils, to be more accurate). The graphite in pencils is stacked sheets of carbon atoms – they simply tried pulling out a single sheet by getting busy with the sticky tape over and over again until it was one atom across. It was exciting stuff: 'Great Scott, it's still three atoms thick, we're out of tape and Staples shuts in five minutes!' That kind of thing. 'I can't find the end! I can't find the end!'

If the hype is correct, and not all hype is correct, this

'miracle material', which is 100 times stronger than steel (the days when we could be impressed by the strength of steel are over), has the potential to create everything from super-strong aircraft to super-strong windows to super-strong plastic to miniature computers and really big touchscreens. Graphene is strong, and highly conductive. How strong? Super-strong. Strong enough for an elephant to balance on a pencil. Who would want to balance an elephant on a pencil? Don't know, but now they can give it a go. Could this elephant spin around on this pencil? Don't know that either.

At the moment they can only make it in tiny quantities. And the race is on to produce graphene in large quantities and make it commercially useful. But graphene (and its new competitor silicene) is just entry-level nanotechnology, a new discipline which, according to its advocates, could be nothing less than a revolution in what stuff can do. You probably thought you could rely on stuff just to be stuff. But that isn't the case. People are starting to muss with stuff in new ways – tiny ways.

The wilder realms of nanotechnology offer sci-fi type scenarios of tiny robots repairing your body from the inside. And there is talk of a new industrial revolution, only this time there shall be no sleeping in factories! (Except maybe in China or somewhere like that.) Nanotech visionaries posit things like a 'post-scarcity material economy' – with machines that can produce literally any object – in a shift analogous to passing from the Stone Age to the Iron Age. Iron is old news. Just like steel.

Alternatively, nanoparticles could just poison us all, or nanorobots could turn the world to goo (literally). So it's the end of scarcity, or the end of everything, or possibly something in between. Of this we can be sure, though: some very small stuff is going to happen.

By the way, graphene pioneer Andre Geim was previously best known for his 'frog levitation' experiment showing how small amphibians when placed between two large electromagnets start swimming in the air.

This is just the kind of decadent fun you'd particularly enjoy if you had spent your formative years under Stalinism, but no way was that going to bag him a Nobel Prize. What were the practical applications? Anyway, he's stopped all that frog shit now.

What is nanotechnology and what the hell does it think it's doing?

Everything ever written about nanotechnology always mentions the 1959 lecture by US physicist Richard Feynman titled 'There's Plenty of Room at the Bottom' in which he posed the question: 'Why cannot we write the entire 24 volumes of the *Encyclopaedia Britannica* on the head of a pin?' (And here it is now, being mentioned.)

The implications were unignorable: if you can put an entire multi-volume encyclopaedia onto the head of a pin, shorter books would be a doddle. Anyway, nanotechnologists (aka the little people) have since taken up Feynman's challenge with zest. In 1989, Don Eigler became the first person to move individual atoms, constructing the letters 'IBM' out of 35 xenon atoms, using the revolutionary scanning tunnelling microscope. (He was being employed by IBM to do this; he didn't just think IBM was cool.)

By 2007, scientists in Haifa, Israel, had placed all 308,428 words of the Hebrew Bible – otherwise known as the Old Testament – onto a half-millimetre square silicon chip, less than half the size of a grain of sugar. This work was dubbed the nano-Bible. Is it easier for a camel to pass through the eye of a needle than to write the Hebrew Bible on half a grain of sugar? Don't know; I'm no theologian.

The term 'nanotechnology' was coined by K. Eric Drexler (of whom, more later) in the 1980s, and independently by Tokyo Science University Professor Norio Taniguchi in 1974. (Drexler promises he didn't cheat.) 'Nano' derives from the Greek word for dwarf; although dwarves are nowhere near small enough to serve as adequate comparison tools here (no offence intended), and nanotechnology means mucking about on the scale of nanometres.

So how small is a nanometre? Well, imagine your arm is a metre (which it is). Now divide that up into a thousand. That is a millimetre. Can you even imagine something that small? No. Well, okay you can. A nanometre is a millionth of that. Start mussing with stuff at that scale and that is nanotechnology – engineering at the molecular level.

Up until now, only nature has been that precise. Well, nature needs to get a fucking load of this shit . . .

If claims are to be believed, carbon nanotubes – really, really small pipes – could efficiently convert seawater into freshwater so solving worldwide water shortages (there is still no salt water shortage). Anti-bacterial nano-silver could help heal wounds (it can already stop socks from smelling – which isn't as good, but is still important). Or we can make long-lasting batteries by dipping ordinary, normal paper into nanotube ink, which sounds made up. That's if they can get it all to work.

Scientists at various universities are now developing invisibility cloaks – transparent carbon nanotube sheeting that can bend surface light around an object to hide it from view. (Admittedly, it can only hide tiny things for now, like a micro-etching of a tank rather than an actual tank.)

Scientists at the Netherland's University of Twente have taken a single molecule car – or nanocar, if you will – on a test drive. The BBC website reported this with the headline: 'Tiny 'car' made from one molecule'. (They were right to put 'car' in inverted commas: it's not a car . . . although it is tiny.)

How can nanotechnology do this? As the excellently named Uzi Landman of the Georgia Institute of Technology explains: 'A reduction in size brings about differences in how familiar laws of physics play out at a small scale'. Different physical laws dominate. Gravity is irrelevant, and things stick to each other naturally.

So metals start operating more like plastics; a small cluster of gold can 'move like an amoeba'. Water becomes as thick as treacle with particles becoming 'sticky' and more attracted to one other. (And buttercups become more like the stars. And trainsets become more like barnacles. And clay becomes more like ham . . .) So, er, it's sort of like magic.

Some of the experiments are bobbins, though. At Cornell University, they have created a guitar out of atoms complete with strings you can play, if not actually hear. What's the point? They would doubtless respond that this is a fun demonstration of nanotechnology's awesome potential. But it isn't fun.

A tiny little guitar with strings so tiny that no human

can ever hear them being played? What's fun about that? It's actually kind of awful.

By the way, Richard Feynman has been hailed as a visionary for his seminal 'small letters' speech – which is fair enough, except it's been pointed out that many of the key ideas had been presaged in science fiction: Ray Cummings's *The Girl in the Golden Atom* featured a subatomic microscope that explored the world inside the atom; in Eric Frank Russell's *Hobbyist* a factory manufactures living organisms atom by atom; Robert A. Heinlein's 'Waldo' has slave hands creating ever smaller replicas of themselves . . .

Whether Feynman knew these stories is uncertain, but a colleague did definitely describe 'Waldo' to him shortly before the 'room at the bottom' talk. (Feynman's next talk warned of the Earth being attacked by an evil space-emperor called Ming. This is quoted far less.)

Anyway, what's with all the small writing? That's not encouraging reading – it's *too small*.

Really, really tiny robots

Nanotech zealots claim it will literally change the world, but so far it has been mainly used to make things like transparent sunscreen, fabric softeners and self-cleaning glass. Great. Plus there is one man in Australia who has made a nano suit that traps your farts. The man, Gilbert Huynh, says: 'I've suffered for years from the emissions of my family, and one cannot keep blaming these things on the dog.'

So: a boon for dog victims of the miscarriage of justice. And a future free to fart for us all.

Our endeavours in nanotechnology so far have been

likened to the cave man's first foray into tools. That is, a bit clumsy and really hairy. But the potential for mussing about at molecular level is huge, and many people are beavering away now on stuff that sounds made up.

Medical nanotech promises titchy-tiny nanobots patrolling your body, reporting back on your health – perhaps issuing instructions on how some exercise might help at this stage or pointing out how 'all day breakfast' does not mean 'every day breakfast', you twat. A healthy message, but from a tiny robot that is too small to see. That is the promise. Ultimately nanobots could fix up their hosts' bodies, forever repairing damaged tissue until, it is claimed, we become virtually immortal. (Yes, the transhumanists are into nanotechnology.)

Highly directed smart pills could transport drugs to affected areas, and nanobots could cook cancer inside the body. Indeed, if nanobots could deliver drugs and do surgery from within, the whole cutting-into-the-skin side of surgery could well be consigned to history and hospital programmes will get a whole lot less gory. The distantly mooted lab on a chip is a tiny, tiny MRI that scans the body and offers instant diagnosis. It doesn't work yet but that's the essence: it's tiny and it diagnoses everything.

Buckyballs (or Buckminsterfullerenes – named after the futuristic architect Buckminster Fuller) are spherical molecules of 60 carbon atoms that could help propel these nanobots about the place. Rice University has invented a nanocar with four buckyballs as wheels, which they hope will push a nanobot around your bloodstream zapping cancer cells as it goes. Nanocars pushing round tiny robots: this would certainly add a certain novelty to the treatment of cancer, which can otherwise lack fun elements. As yet, the car has no engine, so that's a shame.

Rice scientists have successfully used tiny gold-plated 'nanobullets' to help destroy inoperable cancers. So that's nice. Although, as the name suggests, nanobullets might also be used for evil; similar technologies are being explored for the battlefield. In future conflicts, nanobots might destroy weapons or communications systems – or people. According to Dr John Alexander of the US Joint Special Operations University: 'They might be able to punch holes in blood vessels if you want to destroy an adversary.' So that's not nice.

But why stop at just having the battlefields swarming with tiny dust-sized nano-computers sending back info? We could have tiny dust-sized nano-computers sending back info *everywhere*. This is the promise of smart dust. Dust that is smart. Rather amazingly, such a scheme is actually being developed by, wait for it . . . Hewlett-Packard. *Hewlett-Packard!*

In 2009, the computer/printer sleeping giant, the people who hitherto mostly just ripped you off for inkjet cartridges, launched a ten-year project called 'Central Nervous System for the Earth' which ultimately aims to sprinkle the world with over a trillion tiny electronic sensors, gathering information and making observations about people, cities, ecosystems, traffic patterns, energy use, you name it. This is called sensor computing. One day, the Hewlett-Packard (*ha!*) researchers hope a trillion-strong network will cover the world and deliver data to anybody who feels the need for it, from carmakers to governments.

So . . . is this okay? It doesn't sound okay. Did anyone ask them to do this? This is surely worth noting:

Hewlett-Packard, the people who hitherto mostly just ripped you off for inkjet cartridges, are into flooding the world with smart dust to harvest info for sale to the highest bidder. They have told us about it, so there should be no cause for alarm when it happens. Okay? Good.

Wait till you hear what Lexmark are up to.

(I don't actually know what Lexmark are up to).

There's plenty of room for the bottom up

Nanotechnology sounds like it should be very fiddly. It is easy to envisage nanotechnologists forever going, 'Aaah, shit! Almost had it there . . .' But no, that would be wrong, because of atomic tweezers (very, very small tweezers).

But how do they keep tabs on these nano-tweezers? Surely they keep dropping them and not being able to find them? No. These 'tweezers' are about the size of a fridge; it's just the tips that are small. Tweezers that at one end are as big as fridges and at the other as small as atoms: this is the current top-down model of nanotechnology manufacture.

But the big nanotech holy grail is the bottom-up self-assembler, revolutionary machinery that simply makes stuff, any stuff, at the push of a button (before doing away with the buttons and making stuff on their own). This is atom-by-atom construction and modification of literally any object – and it is the dream of the nanotech dreamers.

Also variously called a nanofactory or a molecular self-assembler or a matter printer or a personal fabricator (or any other combination thereof), this is a manufacturing system that produces atomically correct products – vehicles, clothes, computers – made with ultra-strong materials constructed from common elements like hydrogen, oxygen, carbon, nitrogen, aluminium and silicon. All you need to do is pop the design on a computer and hey presto: object.

Whether it is even possible to make such a thing work is disputed, but it doesn't stop people trying. And in the words of US futurologist Joel Garreau: 'If a self-assembler ever does arrive, that's going to be one of history's great holy shit moments.' (History's Great Holy Shit Moments does actually sound like quite a good series.)

The ability to make and have stuff at will, anything we may need, is sort of a final mastery of matter, and will obviously have huge implications – not least for people who make stuff, sell stuff or need stuff. So that's everyone. It's a game-changer.

The nanofactory's earliest incarnation is sort of already here in the form of the 3D printer – working on nowhere near atomic scales, but still no slouch in the vaguely alchemical production of useful stuff. In 2012, Dutch scientists announced a 3D printer had created a transplant jaw for a 83-year-old woman by melting successive thin layers of titanium powder with a laser beam. Being a perfect fit, surgery and recovery times were massively decreased. This is a mighty vision: an elderly generation newly equipped with super-strong jaws, able to munch through even the toughest of biscuits with ease. Even, say, ginger snaps. (The Dutch scientists did not fully explore these implications.)

Coming too are 3D printers for the home. US start-up company MakerBot has just launched the £1,000 Replicator – yes, that is a Star Trek reference – which makes plastic models of anything up to the size of a loaf of bread. So it's the perfect present for anyone who likes plastic models of bread.

MakerBot's chief exec Bre Pettis claimed: 'It's a machine that makes you anything you need. Handy in an apocalypse or just handy for making shower curtain rings and bathtub plugs.'

So it's perfect if you need a bathplug in an apocalypse.

The goo will out

So nanotechnology offers up the teasing, tantalising possibility of being able to make anything at will, and thus ending scarcity. On the downside, there are fears about runaway nanotechnology. Sadly, the 'runaway' in the phrase 'runaway nanotechnology', is not 'runaway' in the romantic, Del Shannon sense. This is 'runaway' in the sense of setting off a runaway change in all things that will really, really fuck us up – a mass of exponentially self-replicating tiny robots that eat the natural environment and turn it into more and yet more of their self-replicating selves until they weigh more than Earth. That kind of 'runaway'. The sort that turns the world to so-called 'grey goo'.

Amusingly, the idea of grey goo, which sceptics use to attack nanotechnology, originated with nano's chief proselytiser K. Eric Drexler, who came up with the idea in his 1986 book *Engines of Creation* and has regretted it ever since. Drexler doesn't even think it's an issue (this thing he himself came up with), and just wishes everyone could be quiet about this idea of his, which was his idea.

'Hey – grey goo guy!' they shout at him in the corridor at conferences. 'Oh, piss off,' he retorts.[4]

Grey goo keys into our fear that anything given autonomy will ultimately turn against us – and our fear of things we cannot see. Things we cannot see turning against us: it's fucked up. Nano, which offers the ultimate mastery of matter, might rise up and master the matter that is us. But there is a possible solution: blue goo. Blue like the police (oh, yes). The goo police; goo that polices goo. Blue goo.

Nano-enthusiast Alan Lovejoy reckons these self-replicating nanobots could keep the nasty grey ones in check, leading to a world 'infested with repair and defence nano-agents, at high density, ready to spring to action'. An 'overwhelming mass' of blue goo 'enforcers' could be 'rapidly imported from a central distribution facility'. The aggressively armed police nanobots would be 'withdrawn from massive floor-to-ceiling ware-houses, wakened and programmed, transported to the site, then slathered atop the infected area as thick as butter on toast'.

This all sounds highly convenient and just sort of made up. But still, nice one. It does raise the question of why the blue goo then doesn't take over, but what the hell.

'Can they be trusted? Subverted?' asks Lovejoy, putting us back at square one, goo-wise. But whatever.

Anyway, there is more to the grey goo debate than the

[4] Along with other nanotechnologists, Drexler (who says modestly of nano-tech that 'I set out to save the world') is obsessed with cryonics – preserving human bodies until nanotech has found the ways to revive and heal them so they can come back and never, ever go away. Jesus, what is up with these people? These guys *hate death!* Whatever happened to making some space, you *egotistical pricks?!.*

mere end of humanity. It is also a fight for nanotechnology's soul. In one corner are the Drexleresque, fantasy-or-nightmare/utopia-or-destruction types, the would-be post-human dreamweavers who believe the nanoscale is a wild frontier to be mastered by the mastery of man, and wax lyrical about touching the atom being basically 'erotic' (Colin Milburn, in *Nanovision*).

In the other, there are the people who just want to make really, really small stuff that's useful. These practical types – the Squares, as they should be called – include people like the US government-sponsored National Nanotechnology Initiative. For them, grey goo is either nonsense and the stuff of sci-fi, or a problem for the far, far future. They think wittering on about erotic immortality or utopian matter printers does nothing but bad for 'real', scientific, evolutionary nanotechnology (getting on with discovering stuff like graphene). And it puts the shits up people.

You have to sort of hope that the wilder side wins out. Not because you necessarily want a mass of exponentially self-replicating tiny robots eating the natural environment and turning it into more and yet more of their self-replicating selves until they weigh more than Earth (aaarrrggghhh!), but because if you're going to do some molecular mad shit, you might as well let rip.

If you're fucking shit up, fuck shit up. That's the clear lesson here. Fuck shit up.

The endless possbilities are limitless
Whether it's mussing about making graphene, or dreaming up machines that master all matter, nanotechnology is a

world of possibility. Or is it a dead end? Or mostly hype? Is it destined, in the words of one critic (David E. H. Jones of Newcastle University), to 'remain just another exhibit in the freak-show that is the boundless optimism school of technical forecasting'? Will it prove to just be a fancy name for normal science doing small stuff? We'll see.

Some people are fearful that regulators won't keep up with nano developments – because they don't understand them and anyway the pace of change is too fast. And already there are concerns of nanoparticles possibly being highly toxic; studies found some carbon nanospheres and nanotubes fatally inflamed the lungs of rodents, damaged fish organs and stunted crop growth. So there are fears of nanoparticles causing asbestosis-type illness. (Although maybe if the nanoparticles cause cancer, nanobullets can cure it – or maybe that's just bollocks.)

Even more worryingly, nanotech might make everything very slippery. Noting the extreme slippiness of some nanospheres, David Rejeski, director of the Woodrow Wilson International Center for Scholars' Foresight and Governance Project, said they could be 'like the nano version of banana peels'. Which might be a laugh at first, but would probably pall over time.

But let's assume these are just teething troubles for the new industrial revolution, the Pot of Gold at the End of the Rainbow to end all Holy Grails. What are the implications of being able to produce whatever you want at will? They are unlikely to be small.

It represents a potential end to scarcity, and even inequality in some sort of true communist utopia. Or does it? Will everyone be able to join in the fun? Will the rich nations let the others have it? And if they don't, won't the world economy collapse in a lopsided way? Will the rich in the rich nations let everyone else in the rich nations have it? Some have even posited a kind of nano-police state, with billions of unseen mini cameras monitoring literally our every move.

And if you can make anything, what stops you making weapons? What stops states, and non-state actors, making a lot of weapons? Fucked up futuristic ones.

In Neal Stephenson's novel *The Diamond Age*, which takes place in a world transformed by nanotechnology, true worth for the wealthy comes to be represented in the organic and hand-made and the old; so maybe elites will always find ways of setting themselves apart. After they've nanoed themselves immortal, maybe they'll start whittling. The nanotech embroidery revival: it's already been mooted. By me.

Companies like IBM and GE are fully engaged in the race to cash in on nanotechnology – so presumably *they* don't think it's the end of capitalism and the world as we know it. Although this would be a rather grand historical irony if, in the race to be first to the nanotech buck, the world's largest businesses end up putting themselves, and everybody else, out of business. One would have imagined capitalism's self-preservation instincts might kick in before that eventuality were it not for the fact that, as pretty much the whole world now appreciates, capitalism's self-preservation instincts do not actually exist.

So we can go round in circles with this stuff for ever. But we cannot ignore it. Well, we can ignore it, because it is very small, but we should not.

In the words of another key nanotech nut, Dr Ralph Merkle: 'It's like nature has given us a load of Lego blocks and we've got boxing gloves on our hands. Nanotechnology is going to allow us to take off the boxing gloves.'

We are like cavemen in boxing gloves, playing Lego. We need to move on.

CHAPTER 6: FOOD

Jelly(fish) and ice cream

Give people soup and they will drink soup. This was categorically proven by Cornell professor Brian Wansink in an experiment using a bottomless bowl of soup – there was a secret tube that kept on refilling the bowl with soup from below – to demonstrate that how much people eat is largely dependent on how much you give them. The group with the bottomless bowl ended up consuming nearly 70 per cent more than the group with normal bowls. What's worse, nobody even noticed that they'd just slurped far more soup than normal.

The bottomless bowl. It's a metaphor and, in this case, an actual bowl.

But do we have a bottomless bowl? An actual one. No, hang on, a metaphorical one. Anyway: how are we going to feed the world?

We face a multiple-whammy of rising temperature, pressure on water supplies, increased consumption from nations becoming wealthier (China and India), possible erosion of arable land by climate change, *and* a rising population – potentially 9.7 billion by 2050 (from 7 billion) on current predictions: that's a big demand for food in a world where already many go hungry (albeit while yet others are obese and shitloads of food is wasted).

Mooted wonder-cure GM provokes public fear. Everyone likes vague fears of things they don't quite understand – it's one of the things that makes us human. But are we right to be scared? After all, the genetic modification people do clone cows. And cows, in and of themselves bring fear to men.

Or is GM just an extension of artificial insemination and cross-breeding – the sort of things that produced a surplus in the first place, and got lots of us off the land and into cities? Should we be concerned by the future of our food being stitched up by corporations who have a mafia relationship with farmers and one of wilful arrogance to everyone else? Or is that good?

Certainly we should look forward to eating some different stuff. With overfishing we could be waving goodbye to cod and haddock. But warmer seas means saying hello to algae – actually, we already eat some algae in the form of sushi seaweed. YO! Algae. That's the future.

Then there're all the jellyfish we'll be eating. And the insects . . .

Look, it's like this: the future will involve looking at many things you have never considered eating before, and wondering if you could eat them. Anemones. Bark. Glue. Wrap it in pancetta. Lovely.

The indestructible sandwich (and other stories)

NASA has recently constructed a bread pudding that can last four years. Yes, bread pudding is changing too. One day soon, we will have bread puddings that will never die. And yes, that is NASA as in the space people.

Meanwhile, the Pentagon has made a pound cake that retains its bounce for five years. This is big news for fans of delayed gratification. And yes, that is the Pentagon that does the wars and stuff.

These bodies are truly getting involved in the food preservation game – they are using cakes for their own ends (often evil ends, sadly). Better, longer-lasting rations for soldiers and spacemen will improve morale and maintain fitness levels. And who would want to face an army full of pound cake? No-one.

A team led by prominent food technologist Lauren Oleksyk, employed by the US Department of Defense Combat Feeding Directorate (which exists), even unveiled the 'indestructible sandwich' – a bread envelope stuffed with pepperoni that can last three to five years without refrigeration. According to *Time* magazine, 'The filling has water-absorbing ingredients that keep it from seeping into the bread and causing moisture damage.' This 'indestructible sandwich' is not indestructible like gold is indestructible. It can be destroyed. And indeed eaten. So it's still recognisably a sandwich of the present.

Even civilians are thinking about making food new, and different, and longer-lasting, and less boring. Naturally, the molecular gastronomy guys are taking on the task of futurising your food with relish.

We have not traditionally considered printers to be appetising, but that will change when printers start printing your dinner. Homaro Cantu of Chicago's feted Moto restaurant is exploring the possibilities of printed food: 'Let's say you have a food printer and eight cartridges, and grow eight crops on the roof, and that's all you need to replicate any food product you can imagine, from mom's apple pie to a cheeseburger with French fries.'

It's as wholesome as mom's printer's apple pie.

The technology already exists. A prototype called the Moléculaire, a French-designed construction, promises 'three-dimensional desserts, complex structures, shapes for molecular dishes, and patterns for decorating a meal.' Three-dimensional desserts: whatever next?

Nanotechnology is looking to get involved with food. Nano additives might mean food that can be altered at will to, say, change colour or be boosted with a particular vitamin.

We should also keep taking our pills. There is already an increasing crossover of the food and drug industries, to produce so-called 'farmaceuticals' (or nutraceuticals): apples that cure headaches; appetite-suppressing toothpaste; breakfast cereals that treat acne . . . the list of truly pointless crap being invented is frankly endless. Vaccine fruit: it's on the way. (As so often, Japan has already blazed a trail here – with a chewing gum that apparently firms up your breasts. It's called Bust-Up. I'm not making that up.)

Researchers in the UK have developed a pill that provides an instant Mediterranean diet: each pill has the vitamins and minerals of six-and-a-half pounds of tomatoes. Anyone currently ploughing their way through six-and-a-half pounds of tomatoes should be greatly relieved (they probably shouldn't be doing that though).

Pills could also be making safe the world of horrible tasting plant-life, which is still most plant-life: through the miracle of the miracle berry. This berry, also known as synsepalum dulcificum, has been used in Africa for centuries to mask acidic flavours. Its essence has been turned into a pill called mberry which transforms sour foods to sweet making digestible all kinds of vegetation previously considered off-limits. Oak leaves. Cactus. Weeds. Lovely.

Perhaps mberry could also help us keep down all the insects we might be munching. According to the Food and Agriculture Organization of the United Nations (FAO), there are an estimated 1,462 species of edible insects. Some experts believe we will start farming insects as an alternative form of protein. They certainly take up less space than cows or pigs. And apparently a pound of grasshoppers is as nutritious as a pound of beef. Can I suggest the marketing slogan: 'It's Insectious!'

But should we be forcing drugs on our kids? Drugs as they are thus far consumed in schools do not generally help with school work or a solid attitude to learning. But we are not talking about recreational drugs – these drugs are educational. For the world of food supplements is to be revolutionised.

One pill makes you larger, and one pill makes you small, and one pill provides you with enhanced cognitive capabilities with which to excel in examination conditions. It's not exactly blowing the doors of perception off their hinges, is it? Drugs to help you blow the doors of perception off their hinges are the past. Drugs to get you a starred A are the future. So it's a bright future for kids who can afford drugs, which is not a statement you read very often.

Ageing populations in wealthier nations will also mean many aged mouths to fill. The food industry is already gearing up to respond to these changing demographics, with experimental mashed-up food in tubes (like for babies), and food that would, say, ward against Alzheimer's – and better aid talking about 'the old days': 'I remember when the iPhone 4S came out in white. People shat themselves with joy . . .'

By the way, in Japan – where the ageing problem is particularly acute – the porn industry has responded with the rise of elder porn – that is, porn by, for and featuring the elderly.

One report on this phenomenon quoted Shigeo Tokuda, the 74-year-old star of such films as *Forbidden Elderly Care* (which sounds like an episode of *Panorama*, but possibly does not look like it). 'People of my age are usually very hesitant to show their private parts,' he admitted.

Indeed, just think of the draughts.

It were all vertical fields round here

Tractors that drive themselves sound fun, but are they? Definitely many believe technology can boost agriculture simply by streamlining its systems and using sensors to regulate crop-spraying and that. And maybe it can.

Others are trying to think of new places to grow stuff – like vertical farms: that is, skyscrapers filled with floors of orchards and fields using soil-free hydroponic or 'aeroponic' methods to produce crops throughout the year. High-rise farms that are like cannabis farms, but which only grow veg: it's already been mooted.

But however we do it, more people on the Earth means we need plenty of produce. Simple as.

Some people argue that we should turn our back on agri-science entirely – shunning it – and turn towards Mother Earth, embracing her. That is, the answer to the world's food problem involves being organic all the time, all the places. (Organic farming now accounts for less than half a per cent of farming.)

They're not just hippies. They're into things like naturally blending strains of wheat or rice, or moving from annual crops to perennials – huge, but not impossible, step changes. But still: you don't have to be an expert to consider this wishful thinking borne of spending too much time outdoors (yes, you can do that). The problem seems to be encapsulated in the question: is there enough room for everyone in the world to have an allotment?

So should we instead bow down to the big corporations? The big corporations think so. Genetically modified food has not done well, public relations-wise, attracting phrases like 'Frankenfoods', which conjures visions of a screwy Germanic scientist, eyes gleaming, having sewed together a succession of corpses, on a stormy night, manically beavering over his contraptions, creating something from nothing – for your dinner. It's not conducive to relaxed snacking. 'Terminator Gene' is slightly offputting too.

The industry doesn't even help itself on the moniker front. The name of the clone made by US biotech firm Cyagra from a prize-winning Wisconsin cow? Vandyk-K Integrity Paradise 2. Okay, Daisy is a cliché, but there has to be something better. Are these cows not human? (No, cows are evil.)

But GM promises much that does at least initially sound fairly appetising. The cassava root is a staple crop for millions – it is cheap and easy to grow, but is currently missing crucial nutrients. Enter scientists, boosting its vitamin and mineral content to create a super-food. Screw five-a-day; hello one-a-week! Boosting nutritional qualities is of particular interest in the developing world, where five-sixths of the world's people live, and all of the malnutrition resides.

With GM, we could make transgenic plants that produce omega-3 oils and allsorts; radically reduce the amount of pesticides needed by making crops resistant to traditional pests; even create plants that can get nitrogen from the air and thus don't need fertiliser – so there's an environmental angle: creating plants that need fewer inputs.

There is understandable unease here, however. A lot of anti-capitalists paint GM giant Monsanto as a big bad corporation of almost stereotypical strong-arming amorality and you think, well, whatever, same old same old. But then you look at how they act.

Monsanto owns an estimated 11,000 patents. They are taking over the food game, by taking over the seeds that grow the food. The seeds are theirs. So the food that comes from the seed is theirs. We are theirs. We are their bitches.

As numerous court documents show, the company sends out small armies of hardball investigators and legal teams to strong-arm any small farmers they believe may be breaking their patents. The company staunchly denies this, but many farmers claim they have been intimidated by Monsanto's 'seed police' after their GM seeds were found growing on their land against the farmers' wishes. Of course, seeds blowing in the wind and propagating the surrounding area is very much the nature of the beast. If you don't like it, stay the hell out of the seed game.

Meanwhile, so-called Roundup Ready crops in Argentina are GMed to be resistant to Monsanto pesticide Roundup, so it can then be liberally sprayed to kill all the bad stuff. But the bad stuff is becoming resistant to Roundup – meaning the importation of nasty old-school pesticides that are so hardcore they're not used in Europe any more.

So it's not good. Then again, of all the bad corporate

science stuff coming along, GM food does at least claim to help in the fight against starvation. If true, that would be an undeniable plus. Also in its favour: it's virulently opposed by Prince Charles, who is a man of anti-science.

Then again, the evidence on increased crop yields from GM is not so great. Every time you buy a seed from Syngenta, Monsanto, or any big GM company, you compulsorily 'agree' that you will not do any comparative trials of this seed against any competitors.

This means the industry has complete control over the trials that are done on its products and so has completely protected itself from peer review – or, to put it another way, science. Shielding yourself from science: that's quite anti-science too.

So it's people like Prince Charles on the one hand versus cartoonishly dodgy corporationy corporations on the other. Which is helpful.

Maybe the GM debate is on shifting ground anyway – what with China merrily GMing away on its own terms. It's been fairly ubiquitous in the USA for years. It's really only Europe that's holding out, with the debate intensifying as a GM second wave wells up.

GM or organic? Or, er, something in between? Others are now pointing to the possibility of genetically engineering crops to make them grow better organically.

Get your head round that, Jonathon Porritt.

To the sea, to the sea

The seas are dying. It's sad, but true. Around 70 per cent of all wild fish stocks are overexploited or depleted. A mere quarter of stocks have capacity for more fishing. But not all marine life is in retreat. Jellyfish are on the attack.

But it's not a bad thing. Like jelly? Like fish? All your boxes should definitely be ticked by jellyfish. Overfishing and rising ocean acidification (from increased carbon in the atmosphere) appear to be letting these gooey monsters of the shallows take over; infestations of 'massive jellyfish' have already closed beaches in Lanzarote, so undermining the island's fairly central tourist industry. Yes, a bit like Jaws, but without any actual jaws.

But what if these wobbly bastards could become some kind of local delicacy? Would the tourists start flooding back? This is truly being proposed by future foodies. True, I have never looked at a jellyfish and thought, 'Wonder what that tastes like?' But then, if I'd never eaten fish before, I probably wouldn't have fancied them much either. Fish often look fucked up.

As regards fish-fish, some say fish farming is the future. But many farmed fish are fed on fish from the seas, which are dying (as we know). To produce one kilogram of decent salmon from a fish farm you need four kilograms of wild fish. So that doesn't work. Unless we substitute yeast-based feed for the wild fish, like Marmite, but for salmon in tanks. Yeast-based feed: fish either love it or hate it.

There's also fish ranching (yee ha!) – huge cages of fish floating in the sea. But people are so far uneasy about semi-farmed fish mixing, and mating, with the so-called real fish. Possibly it's discrimination.

The GM people are pitching in again here with Frankenfish. In a place far away, in a facility behind a high wall, at the top of the Panamanian highlands, there lurks . . . a fucking great big salmon.

That is, in a huge, walled facility in the highlands of Panama they have developed an Atlantic salmon that grows twice as fast because its genes have been augmented with DNA from the fast-growing Pacific Chinook salmon and the eel-like ocean pout, enabling it to eat year round and not just in spring and summer.

Obviously it was immediately dubbed Frankenfish. But it's real name is AquAdvantage® Salmon. Which is actually worse. Here they go with the names again. At least Frankenfish sounds cool. Look out – it's the Rocky Horror Fish! That kind of thing.

AquAdvantage® Salmon feeds on small fish, so there's that problem again. But to avoid contaminating old-school salmon, the super-salmon are kept on land (in tanks; not actually on land-land), and are not allowed to breed.

They have yet to be cleared for human consumption. But will one escape and wreak havoc? Well they are super-fish. So yes.

So watch out.

All the water in the sea might help with another resource issue: water. Water shouldn't be a problem; fresh water falls from the sky all the time. In the words of US physicist Robert B. Laughlin: 'The total precipitation that falls on the world in one year is about one meter of rain, the height of a golden retriever.'

So just imagine every inch of the world covered in golden retrievers. Now imagine that those golden retrievers are not golden retrievers, but water. Now you're getting it.

We are struggling to catch the water with one hand, while turning on the tap with the other. Humans are doing a bad job with the water. We are stupid. Much of it goes back to food, in a way: agriculture uses colossal amounts of wet stuff; it already uses around 70 per cent of all freshwater supplies and a UNESCO report found that the demand from agriculture would rise another 19 per cent by 2050 (such accuracy!).

So it's bad. The problem of droughts is growing. Australians are calling the past ten years the Big Dry, which makes them sound like some half-witted peasant-clan from the post-apocalypse (which is not accurate at all). Somehow it seems wholly fitting – if certainly still unfortunate – that the US city whose future is most at risk from the shortage of water is Las Vegas, a location that has long been associated with pissing it away, idiotically.

In the USA now, separate states are competing over resources – if one actual nation can't sort this stuff out, what about when nations compete against each other? Clearly, a more enlightened attitude is necessary. Having said that, it might be fun to have two villages in, say, Dorset thrust into some kind of organised competition over water resources. Only for a limited period, obviously. And strictly no guns!

Strange as it may seem, technology may actually be of benefit here. Nanotech could be of great use in removing the salt from the seas, which are still very plentiful in water (Saudi Arabia is stepping up research on this). Meanwhile, water filtration techniques are improving the abilities of communities to re-use their water supplies or – to put it another way – drink their own piss. Although there can be a certain resistance here. One recent survey on a Boston radio station found: 'Around 60 per cent of people are unwilling to drink water that has had direct contact with sewage.'

This raises the question: how willing were that 40 per

cent? Being actively willing to drink water that has had direct contact with sewage seems weird. Let us hope they were merely resignedly open to this as a possible solution to the water problem.

I personally think we should go for it and am planning on launching a chain of restaurants called YO! Jellyfish And Piss. Yes, some will be put off by the name but I'm confident it will attract as many people as it repels.

Anyway, drinking your own piss – it's the future.

The challenge of meat

'From an evolutionary point of view, junk food cravings are linked to prehistoric times when the brain's opioids and dopamine reacted to the benefit of high-calorie food as a survival mechanism.'

That's right: our Stone Age ancestors survived on junk food, so a large part of us would like to do the same. Something like that.

Anyway, even more than fish and jellyfish, the future of food revolves around meat. In the words of Paul Roberts, in his book *The End of Food*: 'In a perverse way, the story of the modern food economy now turns back to where it began – with the challenge of meat.' (We must embrace the challenge of meat in a perverse way, or die.)

Meat is a challenge. Give people more and they will eat more. Babies like meat. Give a baby some meat – they will gorge upon it. We all know why. It's proper.

The world likes meat. Fruit and veg are all very important, but people in India and China have had it with fruit and veg. They have had their fill. They want meat.

China is cow mad – importing beef, plus loads of breeding stock from 'countries it trusts', plus experts to show them how to turn some cows into more cows. Where before you imagined China sucking in raw materials from the world – all that wood and stuff – now add in cows. China is sucking in cows. Literally! (Okay, not literally.)

So the world wants meat. But the world's appetite for meat is fucking up the world. Cattle take up nearly a quarter of cultivable land – probably more when they lie down before it starts raining. In the USA, almost 70 per cent of grains and cereals are now fed to animals. Who has eaten up all the cereal? It's the ruddy animals!

Craig Venter is the maverick US genetics guru who headed up the private rival to the Human Genome Project and who in 2010 caused a stir by creating 'synthetic life' (that is, injecting totally new DNA into a living bacterium). Today he eulogises vat meat as crucial in feeding the world more efficiently. It takes 10 kilograms of grain and 15 litres of water to produce one kilogram of beef so, he asks: 'Why not get rid of the cows?'

Beef without the cows. The dream we all dream of. We are talking artificial meat – meat grown in a vat. So-called cultured meat, or in vitro meat, born not of cow or chicken, but of cell biology.

Scientists are beavering away right now trying to whisk up burgers and chicken fillets. One current form grows the muscle cells of pigs in a serum made from cow blood. This meat is then zapped with electricity to 'exercise' it, so providing bulk. Yes, it sounds freaky as all hell. Vladimir Mironov, a biologist and tissue engineer at the Medical University of South Carolina, asks: 'How do you want it to taste? You want a little bit of fat, you want pork, you want lamb? We design exactly what you want.'

But vegetarian pressure group PETA are down with this because it cuts out the slaughterhouses (vat-grown meat is not murder). In 2008, they even offered $1m to the first developers to make it a commercial reality, although this move did reportedly cause a 'near civil war' in the campaign group's office. (It was plastic handbags at dawn.)

The questions raised are deep indeed: is it really meat? This meat is definitely more meaty than, say, Quorn – which is a fungus. But then, is fungus definitely not animal matter? What is meat? *Is* meat? These are the kinds of issues that need tackling here.

One obvious practical question is whether anyone will eat ersatz meat. Early incarnations are likely to be in sausages, pies and other processed foods, to get us used to the idea of stuff that doesn't look like meat anyway (and where our standards are already down on the floor). Considering the dodgy provenance of most meat on sale today, maybe people will prefer meat from a vat. There are no trotters or testes in a vat. (Unless they build special trotter/testes vats, but they wouldn't do that. Would they? No, of course not. Oh, my God, they would. They would so do that. No.)

Anyway, when the PR war begins in earnest I would like to suggest the obvious slogan of 'cultured meat for cultured people', accompanied by a picture of someone (me, say) in a smoking jacket enjoying some cultured meat with a glass of elegant red and a William Faulkner on the go.

In my mind – I mean, the ad – there is some Stilton on its own little table.

Foodageddon

So can we produce enough life-forms to sustain our own life-forms? We are, after all, still basically just life-forms that eat other life-forms. Even vegetarians eat life-forms. Even vegans eat life-forms. No, it's true. Not just the fruit and veg that they throw screaming down their hungry gullets, vegans must also be swallowing human atoms all the time. Vegans are essentially cannibals, in the broadest sense. That's just physics. I digress. (I'm right, though.)

It's worth remembering that it's not all bad. Some places will benefit agriculturally from global warming. And, until recently, things had been improving on the nourishment front. The proportion of people who were undernourished as a total of the population went down from 20 per cent in 1990 to 16 per cent in 2003. Okay, that has stopped of late: commodity price increases in 2007 halted the trend away from undernourishment and put it back in the wrong direction. But that will no doubt turn that back round once the world economy starts firing up again in the next, er . . . actually, forget about that.

But we can and do produce enough food to feed everyone. It's just unevenly distributed. While some parts of the world, or of individual countries, are underfed, others are overfed and a bit porky – and wasting huge amounts of food. The overweight people in the world outnumber the hungry (which means they would outweigh them quite considerably).

We waste 100 million tonnes of food a year. Americans chuck away a third of their fish and seafish, 28 per cent of cereals and 15 per cent of meat. Apparently, the most wasted are dairy products and vegetables. What's up with these fucking idiots? 'Oh God, why did I buy all this cream?! I *hate* cream!!'

So we can feed everyone, environment willing. But human ingenuity has managed to build an economic system which means billions are at the mercy of the smallest of fluctuations in the world markets, and lets those who can pay eat and discard as much as they like. It's a very, very complex system that is also quite spectacularly shit.

So the question is how far we can trust the people who invented this system to sort it all out. You know, the people who factory farm chickens; spray carcases to get every last molecule off them; cram billions of animals into mega-farms; aggressively market products packed with salt and sugar; patent seeds and screw farmers; spray chemicals everywhere; put 'pink goo' in burgers etc. – how can we *not* trust those people to sort out the nosh situation?

Some people ardently believe we won't solve the food issue and that, given what they see as inevitable enviro-collapse and social chaos, we're all fucked. In his book *Living in the End Times*, enthusiastic public speaker Slavoj Žižek states: 'We are entering a period in which a kind of economic state of emergency is becoming permanent, turning into a constant, a way of life.' Yeah: fucked economy, fucked ecosphere. Fucked. Get over it. So that's fun.

The most immediate question this raises is: should we bury tins? This is an important point. Some people have started burying tins. Not in their gardens. That would be too obvious. But other places. (Probably somewhere in the local park.)

The Preppers are a growing US movement that believes it is better to be safe than sorry because you have no tins.

This movement has been dubbed Survivalism Lite (you know, preparing for the apocalypse without getting too muddy). There are now prepping courses and conferences. (What are the canapés at a prepper conference? Racoon?)

One prominent prepper John Milandred claimed: 'We get inquiries from people from all walks of life. We had a principal from a school asking us to talk to their children.'

He doesn't mention the other requests not to talk to their children.

CHAPTER 7: COMPUTERS

My laptop can read the future

Google are building a super-computer that, with no hint of irony, company co-founder Sergey Brin likens to HAL from *2001*.

But, says Brin, 'hopefully it would never have a bug like HAL did where he killed all the occupants of the spaceship . . .'

Yes, let's hope not Sergey, you mad bastard.

Anyway, computers keep getting more powerful – so powerful maybe that they develop oracular powers. A University of Illinois project is making great claims that its big digital baby predicted the fall of Egypt's President Mubarak, which led to headlines like 'Super-computer predicts revolution'. Let us skirt around the word 'revolution' being used about an event that leaves the army in control of the country; this computer decided – by instinct? Common sense? What? – that Mubarak was going to fall even as the US government was supporting him, believing they were backing the right horse. The computer out-intuited the US government.

How did it do this? It read the news. Not just some news. All the news. This computer loves the news. It devours all the news. It's hungry for news. It eats news for breakfast. You might read a couple of the Sunday papers. This computer has read all the Sunday papers. It has a great appetite for current affairs. It even reads tabloids 'ironically'.

The computer wonder also honed in on the location of Osama Bin Laden, thanks to media reports of his whereabouts, to 'within 200km'. And yes, okay, as it transpired, he was residing in a central-casting baddie hideout that virtually screamed 'He's in here!' But still, when a computer can read all the news and start to intuit things from that, something is clearly afoot.

But can we really make machines that are clever in the ways that we are? Why are people so fascinated with trying to replicate our intelligence anyway?

And if we do make intelligent machines, will they leave us behind in some massive technological forwards charge? Or can we get the ultimate boost from super-computers – and merge with them, somehow uploading our consciousness to them and thereby living for ever, in the so-called Singularity? Or is that idea just a stream of hot bollocks?

What is consciousness anyway? And is it all that?

The games people play

In a measure of just how fast things have moved, it was only the early 1970s when Hubert Dreyfus (cool name) was writing a book famous in computing circles, *What Computers Can't Do*, arguing that computers would always be fairly mediocre chess players.

Pretty soon, a computer beat Dreyfus, a philosopher with a keen interest in artificial intelligence, at chess – something he bitterly recounted as inspiring 'glee' in the computer community. (They love shit like that, the computer community.)

Similarly, chess world champion Garry Kasparov, one of the greatest chess players ever to grace the squares, once mused: 'The way things are, I can beat any computer, if I concentrate on the computer's style of game. The computer can calculate billions of moves, but is lacking intuition.'

Of course, Kasparov was very famously beaten by IBM's Deep Blue computer in 1997, inspiring headlines the world over: COMPUTER BITES MAN. GRAND MASTER IS GRAND LOSER. And COMPUTERS TO RULE THE EARTH: FLEE.

Meanwhile, right now at Edinburgh University, in Edinburgh, they've built an AI robot that plays Connect 4. The robot – which surreally doesn't have a name – has a camera for an eye to see the moves, and a limb to move the pieces. Connect 4 is surely a step backwards from chess, unless there are more subtleties to the game than initially meets the eye. ('I have noticed his style of play tends towards diagonals . . . cunning, very cunning . . . but not cunning *enough!* Four! Ha! I got four!') Next, the researchers are working on a computer that plays Snap.

Meanwhile the humans had to take another hit in 2011 when a computer called Watson won the US TV game show *Jeopardy!* That a computer could master a logical game like chess or Connect 4 seems essentially fitting. But Watson – embodied as a rectangular flatscreen standing behind a podium – could understand the complexities and puns of modern language and filter general knowledge faster than two past *Jeopardy!* champions.

Puns and general knowledge: that's humanities.

Humanities! The clue's in the name: it's *our stuff!* This was big news and naturally the victory caused much Internet chatter about the demise of the humans. (This chatter, it should be pointed out, came from humans communicating via the Internet, not from the Internet itself.)

Watson had been trained for four years – and required phenomenal amounts of programming and memory to undertake this very singular mission (he ingested the equivalent of 200 million pages of info). Even in the months preceding the show he would still think, for example, that the phrase 'give a Brit a tinkle' meant 'urinate on an Englishman'. So a lot of work went into this.

And being a *Jeopardy!* champ does not suddenly make Watson one of the guys. As Stanford AI scientist Noah Goodman pointed out: 'If you say, 'Watson, make me dinner,' or 'Watson, write a sonnet,' it explodes.' (Actually, that's a slight exaggeration: if you ask Watson to write a sonnet, it just doesn't write a sonnet.)

And while Watson could handle questions like 'If you're one of these capable fellows, you're unfortunately master of none', he would have no response to the question 'What are you going to spend the prize money on?' He wouldn't have a clue! He didn't even go out afterwards and get fucked up.[5]

Anyway, one of the people Watson beat, former champion Brad Rutter, a \$3.2m winner on the show, was gracious

---

[5] One contestant on a Chinese dating game show famously caused a moral panic across the nation when she declared she would rather 'cry in a BMW than laugh on bicycle'. What would Watson rather do? He wouldn't have a clue! (I would, for the record, probably prefer to cry on a bicycle, but that's just me.)

enough to say that, as Watson was built by humans, Watson's victory was still a victory for humanity. (That was in public; in private, he said Watson was 'a cunt'.) (He didn't really say that.)

So what have we learnt? Well, that computers are getting much more powerful and that the goalposts can move. But while all this game playing has shown that what previously had been considered hard – the computational 'thinking' bits – can often be achieved by sheer brute force computing, it has also shown the limits.

Deep Blue was good, but also, at the end of the day, just a fucking great big computer that could only play chess. IBM even went so far as to call their own computer 'stupid'. Which is rude, but you can see their point.

Watson was up front a screen with a globe on it that spoke in an obviously computer-generated voice (computer-generated voices are thus far always obvious) – but there were ten large fridge-size cabinets tucked away out the back. He could out-'think' and out-fact the other contestants, but they could walk up stairs and recognise each other's faces. Could Watson? No.

And to really see what Watson's got in the overtaking humanity stakes, it seems only fair for him/it to try his 'hand' at other shows. *Deal or No Deal*, perhaps. *Or Dancing on Ice*. Then we'll see!

Strong AI vs weak AI: which is the strongest?

It's wrong to assume that all researchers into AI are driven by the crypto-orgasmic obsession with making a man. Those are just the ones that get all the headlines. Some just want to do whiz-bang computing that delivers cleverer air traffic systems or emergency response control centres. Sort of AI-powered thinking systems that do this complicated shit better than we can.

This latter is sometimes called weak AI – as opposed to strong AI, which genuinely tries to replicate human-like thinking. (Although personally I believe that the weak AI people do want to create a man really, but have learnt to cloak their intentions.) (Honestly – watch these people.)

Weak AI involves building computers that can work independently – and make decisions – but without any pretence that this is proper thinking, or true consciousness. It exists in Google algorithms. (Artificial intelligence helping us find decent plumbers: it's already happened.) Then there are the autonomous cars that can drive around the streets by themselves. Or the financial sector constructions that helped bring about the current never-ending misery and woe of the recession. (Best not let those ones behind a wheel.) People are developing AI systems for everything from alleviating traffic congestion to decision-aiding in disaster relief scenarios.

Occasional global calamity notwithstanding, this is all to the good, and testament to the fact that computers are very good at computing stuff, and useful generally. It's also a recognition that there are different aspects to intelligence, and that some can be neatly summed up in an algorithm. But really, who gives a shit about that when you can try to make a man? People have dreamt of making a man at least since the Greeks. Strong AI – or death!

Humans have a strange fascination with intelligent machines. We are bored with the animals. We want machines that we can talk to and we want them now. We were long ago promised properly intelligent super-computers turning on their human creators and needing to be shut down and they did not arrive. The very first conference on AI, in 1956, declared full AI to only be a few years away. The Stanley Kubrick classic *2001: A Space Odyssey* was set (if memory serves) in 2001, a year that did go down in history, but not for an AI computer catapulting his spacecraft's crew member into the vacuum of deep space on a manned mission to Jupiter. That didn't happen.

But we have been obsessed with the idea of these 'computers' (if you will) doing more than computing ever since humans started messing about with computational devices. Soon after legendary IT pioneer Alan Turing had finished his problem-solving machine to defeat Hitler he was asking, in his seminal 1950 paper 'Computing Machinery and Intelligence', whether machines could think. This paper spawned the so-called Turing Test which seeks to discover whether a computer can fool a human. At this point, Turing believed, computers would demonstrably be as clever as humans.

An annual competition held in the UK, the Loebner Prize, seeks to find whether this Rubicon has yet been crossed. Human judges talk to humans and to computers (unseen to them) via instant messaging, and if more guess wrong than right (i.e. the computer fools them it's human) the winning computer seizes the prize yelling: 'AT LAST!! I HAVE DEFEATED YOU AND NOW YOU SHALL PAY!!!! WAH-HAHHAHAHA!' That kind of thing.

So far, it hasn't happened. A computer has never scooped the top prize. This is because when asked, 'Are you a computer?' the computers always say: 'Yes, I am a computer . . . d'oh!' (Not really, they are actually cleverer than that.) Meanwhile, *Wired* columnist Charles Platt managed to bag the annual Most Human Human prize (being the human the Loebner judges thought was least like a machine) in 1994 by being deliberately 'moody, irritable and obnoxious.' Is this not humankind *in excelsis*?

Anyway, even those who hold Turing in great esteem find this test a narrow measure of machine intelligence. Here you are, a mass of transistors able to achieve computational brilliance far beyond the ken of mortals and you are making small-talk with some tosser who keeps trying to catch you out for not sounding human enough. I don't know why they even bother entering.

Many believe simply imitating human chat – passing yourself off, unseen, as human – is not even the same as replicating the human. A computer can say any old shit having been programmed to do it, without really 'understanding' it in any real sense. A computer could converse in Chinese, say, just by flicking through a database of Chinese, with no real understanding of what it is 'saying'. So even if a computer does win – and the closest one got was in 2008, when a computer fooled a quarter of the judges – it will hardly be the end of the matter. What about consciousness? What about empathy? What about all the other things that go along with our ability to chat? What about being able to tell the difference between an apple and a tomato? We must be able to tell apples from tomatoes. It's important!

Despite all this, computers do evidently have strengths that we lack: in 1940, Turing buried some silver bars near Shenley. He tried to find them again on three separate occasions – in 1944, 1946 and then again in 1952 – but came away empty-handed. A computer wouldn't do that. A computer wouldn't mislay its treasure.

Similarly, humans persecuted Turing for being gay. A computer wouldn't do that either.

Or would it?

Conscious of consciousness

The brain has 10 billion neurons, each of which is connected, on average, to about 10,000 other neurons. It is fantastically complex stuff that philosopher Matt Carter likens to a shitload of string being spread around India:

> 'Imagine taking a country the size of India – which has a population of about a billion – and giving every man, woman and child a thousand pieces of string with instructions to find a thousand distinct people to hold the other end of each piece of string. When the whole country is connected up like this, with every person connected to a thousand other people by pieces of string, multiply the whole system in complexity by an order of magnitude and *that's* how complex your brain is.'

So it's not surprising it's difficult to replicate human-style thinking in a computer. But when we do have computers that can operate in ways like the brain, or thereabouts, will they be like us? Or be like something else?

Can computers have minds like ours? Are we just meat machines, inherently replicable given enough computing oomph of the right sort, or have we got something else about us? A certain *je ne sais quoi* that the machines will never attain? Is trying to make computers into 'beings' one massive category error?

Most prominent thinkers on 'consciousness' (our 'experience' of 'thinking' and 'feeling') believe all our thought processes are a material function of our brain, that everything is somehow explained in the wet, porridgy thing in our heads. (Others, of course (religious people – but not just religious people), believe in extra bits of us, like souls and whatnot. Yet others just throw up their hands and say they don't know.)

At one extreme is philosopher and radical atheist Daniel Dennett, who reckons our brains are digital anyway, a highly sophisticated sets of zeroes and ones – trillions of digital gates forever opening and closing in a way that only appears to approximate 'consciousness' (sometimes). Thus he argues that as soon as a computer is telling a zero from a one, it is thinking. 'The best reason for believing that robots might some day become conscious is that we human beings are conscious, and we are a sort of robot ourselves,' he claims.

This is one formulation. It pisses people off. People don't like being told they are robots. They like sunsets, for crying out loud! But could we not be robots programmed to like sunsets? Anyway, you don't have to think brains are digital to think they are more or less a machine.

Nicholas Humphrey, the evolutionary psychologist and philosopher, thinks sunsets are really cool, and tries to claim some idea of 'the soul' (not an immortal one) for science and materialism. For him, consciousness is an extraordinary show we put on in our own heads to make ourselves feel special and transcendent, a sense of wonder to make us want to go on and survive and evolve and do ambitious stuff. So it's sort of a trick of evolution, but a really, really good one and a cause for celebration. This makes us sound less like robots – unless robots really dig very red tomatoes and particularly lovely brooks (maybe they do?). Consciousness, on this formulation, is 'like falling in love', the soppy bugger.

Whatever – we know so little about the brain (we don't even know how neurons work) that people are now trying to reverse engineer the brain, which is tricky, the brain being hard to study as they tend to be inside people's heads and people tend to be using them. It might help in the development of AI. It will definitely help us understand the brain.

Meanwhile, AI researchers keep plugging away making a man. There are lots of different schools of thought taking different approaches. But broadly the thinking now is to try to model the development of AI more on our development of I – embodied, evolving in the real world . . .

But the AI people go on. Say to them, we are unique as we have evolved over millennia – and they will build machines that make computer code compete in a survival of the fittest contest.

Say that we learn in the real world, and they will build robots that learn their way around by trial and error.

Say that our emotions are central to our intelligence, and they will build machines that learn to identify dangers and will call that 'fear'.

Say that computers don't think like brains, and they will build artificial neural networks that attempt to ape the structure of brains.

Say that they are still not like real brains, and they will start wiring up neurons from animals.

Say their creations do not look like a man, and they will start sewing bits of a man together and cackling to the heavens. (They really do do that.)

One AI researcher, a former games software pioneer called Steve Grand working in his garage in Somerset, has symbolised the attempt to evolve an artificial man as we have evolved from apes, by sticking a rubbery monkey face on a metal robot and calling it Lucy.

This creation can sometimes distinguish different types of fruit. No, this is not such an achievement – or is it? Maybe being able to distinguish between different types of fruit is what consciousness is all about.

But still, what could better symbolise evolving something new like we evolved from apes than sticking a plastic ape face onto a tin-can robot?

Forwards to the cosmic infogasm?

Are we just pussy-footing around here, though, blinded by the fact that true AI has not come to pass from realising that it is inevitable and that the onward march of computing will continue unabashed and unabated until we can barely understand what they are doing, and we just need the imagination (whatever that is) to see it?

This is the idea behind the Singularity, an amorphous idea that takes up an awful lot of time and energy in the field of futurology and can elicit erotic reactions in geeks.

Broadly, it's a titanic leap forward in technology that takes things to a level we cannot now comprehend. Which sounds vague.

For some, it is when we upload our consciousness into machines and do away with our shitty old earthly bodies. Which sounds like religion. For others, it is the point where self-replicating computers spread out across the universe, drawing energy from it, until all the universe is a computer. Which sounds like shit fiction.

Basically, if it happens, whatever it is, everything changes – *Homo sapiens* as currently incarnated will be but a 100,000 year stepping stone towards a whole new thing. Papa's got a brand new bag – he's merged with a super-computer to live for ever with as many robot bodies as he likes. It's the end of the world as we know it, because we have become one with our super-computers in an ill-defined, but still utterly inevitable cosmic infogasm, and I feel fine.

The term Singularity was coined by computer scientist Vernor Vinge (pronounced to rhyme with 'dingy') who suggested four possible routes to bring about the post-human era:

1. Building a massive super-computer that is essentially 'awake' (the Check Our New ... Oh Shit! No! NOOOOO! scenario).

2. Networks of computers banding together and 'waking up' (the You Didn't Realise We Were Attaining Consciousness When You Were Playing *World of Warcraft*, Did You? scenario).

3. Humans merging so intimately with their computers that the resultant combo could reasonably be

called superhuman (the I'm My Computer, My Computer Is Me, How Superheroically Happy We Can Be scenario).

4.   Biotech boosters push the humans up to the next level (the I Feel Like Superman When I Take All My Pills scenario).

So he is keeping his options open. When hypothesising about this event horizon in his epochal 1993 article 'The Coming Technological Singularity: How to Survive in the Post-Human Era', Vinge said: 'I'll be surprised if this event occurs before 2005 or after 2030.' (Well, he was right about the first part anyway – so he's 100 per cent correct so far.)

These days, the idea's greatest proponent is Ray Kurzweil, a perma-tanned futurology guru who appears to possess a near-insane urge to avoid death (he takes 250 supplements a day). Kurzweil has co-founded the Singularity University, an academic institution in Silicon Valley (major funders: Google and NASA) which aims to 'assemble, educate and inspire a cadre of leaders who strive to understand and facilitate the development of exponentially advancing technologies and apply, focus and guide these tools to address humanity's grand challenges'.

Bet they're a right laugh.

Anyway, Kurzweil is confident machines will seem convincingly human by 2029 and is currently putting the Singularity at 2045. Kurzweil claims that because computer power is increasing exponentially, at some point The Curve, which is also sometimes called The Spike (there are many portentous capitals in post-human thinking), will turn nearly vertical. (If computer power keeps doubling every 18 months – so-called Moore's Law – the leap each time just gets bigger and bigger to the point that it's really very big indeed.)

We should apparently listen closely to Kurzweil because his predictions have been proved correct many times before – in the late 1980s, he predicted the Internet, which let's face it, has happened. Although actually, his predictions are not always wholly correct. In a TED talk he presented in 2006, he predicted that by 2010 computers would be invisible. As we now know, 2010 was not the year that computers became invisible (they remain, broadly speaking, visible). So we'll see.

But Kurzweil really, *really* needs to see this. We will be able to escape the limitations of being an animal as Darwin described ('the human has beaten evolution,' says Kurzweil). If your brain is in digital form, Kurzweil says you can have as many bodies as you like. The possibilities for the sin of Onan here are truly overwhelming. Kurzweil wants this so much. Not to have a robot orgy with himself. Well, not that specifically.[6]

This Singularity business sounds religious, of course. AI expert Mitch Kapor even calls the Singularity 'intelligent design for the IQ 140 people'. But maybe it will happen?

Or maybe not. Maybe computers won't keep on developing as fast as they have; maybe there is a limit. There has been with other technologies. As Cyperpunk author

---

[6] Clearly, if Kurzweil was a character in a science fiction story, he would finally attain his life's ambition of ever-lasting life by downloading his consciousness onto an immortal computer, and the realisation of what he had lost would drive him out of his mind – thus providing a salutary lesson for all mankind.

Bruce Sterling pointed out: 'Electrical power networks, oil pipelines, water networks. None of these are accelerating out of control.' Maybe computing power will level off in the same way, or at least slow down (definitely there is a limit to how small silicon technology can get, though the nanotechnologists claim to have substitutes waiting in the wings). Maybe the software won't be able to keep up.

There may well prove to be insurmountable problems to downloading an individual human 'consciousness' onto a computer (incredible as that might seem). Without our 'wet stuff' – our brains – perhaps we will only ever be simulacra of proper beings, ineffably processed tracings of what once was . . . and yes, vinyl does sound better than MP3, if you have a good enough record player. Another possibility missed by Kurzweil and his ilk: that the hyper-intelligent machines will not want to merge with freaks like them. Who could blame them?

And if somehow we can merge with the computers and live for ever should we even want to do that? Living forever diffused across some spectral computer world. Is that good? What would you *do* all day? And sorry, but humans who have literally removed the deadline spells one thing: a terrible horror show of procrastination. It's bad enough even *with* death a constant shadowy presence forever breathing down your neck.

One thing is certain. The sort of people who want to merge with computers and live for ever; the sort of people who are actively developing computers so they can do that; those people need to be kept an eye on. No messing.

We have already made a man

Maybe we *are* all computers, but we're not those sort of computers – the ones with plugs and chips and that. Or maybe we shall be saved by the so-called 'wet stuff' in our brains (AI people do call it wet stuff) and the whole central nervous system side that makes us feel proper pain and pleasure. Unless the machines can develop computer hangovers, or computer curry highs, or computer nasty gashes on the head, or computer orgasms (sorry), then these computers' lives will not be worth living.

But, for now, the computers are moving on apace. Can we keep up? Robotics expert Rodney Brooks says robotics and AI are the 'tsunami that will toss our lives into disarray'. And he's one of the people who are into it. As the machines arise, Ray Kurzweil gives humanity 'a 50% chance of survival. But then, I've always been accused of being an optimist' – and okay, he's mental. Marvin Minsky, another AI pioneer, believes that humans are so crap at writing computer software that the first true AI will be 'leapingly, screamingly insane' – so it's all our fault if it goes a bit HAL.

Certainly there is a possible convergence of technologies here that could amount to a tide washing over humanity. If the Singularity freaks are right, will the computers outstrip us so far that we are left flailing in their wake, and will they come 'alive' somehow and go on without us? Or will we get to merge with them and go along for the ride? It doesn't sound like the sort of thing that will happen soon. But that does not necessarily mean it is total cobblers.

Of course, a world of some people with more computers in, on and around them than other people is, yet again, a future rosier for some than others. Human society is almost incredibly unequal now – even before the computer enhancements. Any more would just be taking the piss.

Hyperbole aside, let's not start having posthumanist nightmares just yet. Current attempts at AI look funny and speak funny and use a titanic amount of computing power to do not very much. Ironically, one thing that comes out of the efforts to render our consciousness understandable and finally untangle all the notions of mind and brain, is just how complex and amazing we are. We don't always seem complex and amazing, but we are.

All the things we wonder about – creativity, imagination, unconscious elements of thinking . . . rather than being rendered prosaic by science, seem even more unique and mysterious. Even really bad paintings that you can't believe are going for £450 are the product of processes that are still beyond our greatest minds to explain.

We genuinely don't know how we do it. And the human brain remains, unless aliens tip up with far more advanced consciousnesses than ours, the most highly evolved entity in the universe.

So for now: fuck you, Watson.

CHAPTER 8: SPACE

Space, the final fronter – for privatisation

Space is the new family china, being hawked out to the highest bidder.

In May 2012, the private space company SpaceX successfully sent an unmanned Dragon capsule up to the International Space Station in a move that has been called 'a momentous step towards the privatisation of space'. This experimental freight mission was carrying supplies including water, food, clothes, batteries and – apparently – laptops. Laptops? Did the astronauts on the ISS forget their laptops? It's easily done. '3 . . . 2 . . . 1 . . .' 'Hang on – I forgot my laptop!'

SpaceX was formed in 2002 by one of the guys who invented PayPal – not the scary right-wing PayPal inventor who is funding schemes for genetic enhancement – that was Peter Thiel. This is Elon Musk, who sounds like a fragrance for men, but is actually a billionaire space entrepreneur who is unafraid of using Internet-related gains to step in where actual states increasingly cannot afford to tread.

Do we stand on the verge of an era of mass space tourism leading ultimately to the colonisation of other worlds by humanity, the discovery of boundless minerals and limitless energy and thus the salvation of all? Are we, as some would have it, hovering right up against this verge, about to topple over it? Well, there might soon be a hotel in space: so who knows?

But can we exploit space for monetary gain? Otherwise, what's the point of it?

And is going further into space simply part of our questing destiny: the furthest shore, the final frontier, the search for the new world(s). To outline the continuity in developing ever more ingenious 'craft', they even put a bit of the *Mary Rose* (a sail mechanism) on the last flight of space shuttle *Endeavour*. And yes, Henry VIII's flagship did sink on its maiden voyage, failing to conquer even the Solent – but is the symbolism any less potent for all that? We were *born* to conquer space. Even though space is highly inhospitable. O, my America, my Newfoundland, without any air or natural food supplies.

By the way, the Dragon mission was originally aborted one second before take-off due to technical difficulties. The whole thing had to begin again a few days later, which is one in the eye for those who still claim that privatised space missions are inevitably more efficient than public sector ones.

You save by getting to skimp on employees' pensions though, so it's swings and roundabouts.

Whither the state space programmes

Latterly state space programmes have mouldered. Bunging some of your citizens into space is still a matter of national prestige – it's the reason China sent up its first taikonauts in 2003, and why Italy remains the seventh biggest spender on space (by percentage of GDP), just ahead of Belgium (Belgians in space: it's already happened). But public sector space programmes are still a sorry scene.

Even NASA, having decided to mothball the Space Shuttle, won't have any craft capable of taking people into space, which to the untrained eye would seem to defeat the basic object of being NASA. The Americans will thus be reliant on the Russians to ferry them up to the giant International Space Station. This makes the Russians laugh their big Russian laughs.[7]

The ISS itself – a vast, modular orbiting structure the first parts of which were launched in 1998 – remains unfinished. Late and over budget, lots of the planned experiments have had to be canned as the money had been given to the private contractors who built it, so it's a bit like PFI – which conjures the image of Gordon Brown in space.

You can see the ISS in the night sky with a telescope (or as a dot with the naked eye – whizzing past at 17,000mph (from horizon to horizon in five minutes)). It is staffed by an international crew (the clue's in the name there) of around 30 people. All those nationalities up there, spinning round the Earth, confined: imagine the petty rows. With so many cultures cramped in together, but supposed to be on their best diplomatic

[7] NASA Associate Administrator Bill Gerstenmaier tried to sidestep this new reality by declaring archly: 'We've got a lot of detailed plans that we've been working in-house quietly with technical teams, really building a pretty strong strategy on how we go forward.' Yes, he's bullshitting. That much is clear.

behaviour, it's got to be a passive aggressive nightmare. ('I'm not accusing anyone, I'm just saying that I definitely left some dried veg powder in here.' 'Maybe it floated off.' 'Yeah – floated off into your mouth, you fat American fuck.') ('I left some asteroid samples here.' 'What? Those little bits of rock? I thought they were rubbish so I put them in the rubbish shute and fired them right out into space.' 'What? They took me ages to collect, you arsehole.' 'Look, man – tidy space station, tidy mind – that's all I'm saying.')

Obama even cancelled George W. Bush's grand space programme: to land human beings on the very surface of the moon. Yes, think about that: humans! On the surface of the moon! And okay, that has actually been done before, which is one of the main reasons it was cancelled. And, yes, we have sent a lot of rovers into space – Voyager 1, launched in 1977, is now 120 astronomical units (18,000, 000, 000 kilometres) from the Earth and counting – but if it's left to actual nation states, few of your actual humans would make it 'up there'.

But luckily, the venture capital elites (them again) are filling the void. Space entrepreneurs are already feverishly busy organising day trips to space (due to blast off imminently), with moon tourism being predicted to follow not far behind.

Incidentally, having left the solar system around the height of the Britpop era, in late 2011 NASA announced that Voyager 1 was now entering a new region – a stagnant zone between our solar system and proper interstellar space that it called 'cosmic purgatory'.

That is NASA calling it that. Voyager 1's own feelings on the region are unknown.

But we went to space last year!

Humanity's mavens in the field of private space gubbins are the PayPal guy, Richard Branson, the bloke who set up Amazon, the bloke who invented the computer game *Doom* (I'm not making this up), and a Las Vegas-based hotelier called Robert Bigelow (that's not a euphemistic way of saying he's in the mob)

Bigelow wants to build an inflatable hotel in space called Nautilus (inflatable spacecraft take up less space on the launch vehicle than hard components, so are cheaper). His aim here is to produce a hotel where no one can pop out for a bottle of wine, and absolutely has to use the minibar. There are no shops in space. Not yet, anyway. I mean: just imagine the minibar prices at a hotel in space.

Day trips to space will start soon – spending an astronomical amount of money to whiz just out of 'the sky' and into 'space' (shooting out just over the border, 50 miles up, and briefly experiencing weightlessness) so you can come back down to Earth and proudly declare: 'I have barely been to space!' Already signed up are property developers the Candy Brothers and, er, Buzz Aldrin.

History records the first space tourist as one Dennis Tito, an American investor who paid a reported $20m to ride to the ISS in the spare seat on a Russian supply vessel. But he wasn't the first space tourist at all: Russian space workers had apparently already been letting their mates go to space in the spare seat, for kicks – like a lorry driver taking his son on a half-term jaunt to Belgium. In this, if nothing else, money can't buy you everything; sorry, Dennis. Good name, though, Tito – evoking both a Yugoslav dictator and a member of The Jacksons. Nice one.

In early 2012, Simon Cowell announced his intention to send a winner of *Britain's Got Talent* into space. Which conjures the image of Ashleigh and Pudsey, the dancing dog, in space.

As well as Tito (good name that; Dennis also – evoking Dennis Wilson out of the Beach Boys and Dennis fire engines), Canadian Cirque du Soleil founder and baldy Guy Laliberté has spent time on the ISS, becoming 'the first clown in space'. Laliberté did actually put on a one-man 'artistic production project, an original one' up there – designed to highlight the world's need for clean water. Bet it was quite a spectacular in its own way, but still just fundamentally quite shit. It apparently had a video cameo from Bono (for fuck's sake). 'I see stars, I see darkness and emptiness,' said Laliberté. Yep, that sounds like space.

Bigelow's hotel is due to open for business in 2016 – although you know how these hotels-in-space timeframes can slip. A Russian company is also developing a space hotel (called Hotel in the Heavens and pencilled in for 2016, it would have seven guests at a time). So it's like the Cold War, only for hotels in space.

If you think a hotel in space would be a bit rubbish – all that food out of tubes and floating weightlessly rather than lying on a nice soft bed and that (and God knows how the swimming pool would pan out) – bear in mind that space food has moved on in leaps and bounds since the 1960s; it's quite tasty now apparently. Actually, most of the food might be taken up from Earth and microwaved, and there may not even be any booze (boo!). But the real food up there is love. As the science writer (and viscount) Adrian Berry explains in his book *The Next 500 Years*: 'One of the great joys of the 21st century will be taking holidays in lunar hotels for the specific purpose of making love.'

Space, the final frontier, for the specific purpose of making love.

But wouldn't it get boring? You know, after the novelty has worn off? (That's the novelty of being in space, not cosmic nookie.) Like being on a cruise ship that doesn't stop at places of historical/touristical interest? Or just like being in Centre Parcs generally?

Yes: you would get to see the Earth from space. I would like to see that. I'll admit it. Those who have seen our fragile and beautiful planet from space report a much changed outlook – the view makes us look up, smell the coffee, understand that we should, as a species, care for our homeland.

Although if everyone has to go into space to achieve their green epiphany, that could be quite costly, energy-wise. You know, just to get people to turn their taps off and that.

By the way, as well as PayPal money going into adventuring in space, it's going into nutso libertarian colonies on the high seas (which is like space, only wetter). Peter Thiel is chucking money towards a plan, along with the grandson of Milton Friedman, to develop new floating city-states on stilts in the open seas in a new way of living they call 'seasteading'.

Forget start-up companies. This is about start-up countries. In the middle of the fucking sea. Of which you can sort of be a dictator. With no minimum wage. Or welfare. Or tax. Or even much in the way of gun laws. (So if all Thiel's plans come to fruition, he could escape both death *and* taxes.)

'There's a history of a lot of crazy people trying this sort of thing,' explained another billionaire backer, Joe Lonsdale. 'The idea is to do it in a way that's not crazy.'

Indeed it is.

You want the moon on a stick, you do

The moon might not look like somewhere you'd want to live, but actually it is. There are a lot of minerals up there, like helium 3 that would be great for cheap nuclear fusion. And all that cheese (check fact). The issue of exploiting the moon even entered the race for the 2012 Republican candidature when Newt Gingrich announced his wish to mine the moon. This was a very pro-science stance for someone who struggled with evolution. Challenged that his plans were grandiose, he said: 'I accept the charge that I am grandiose and that Americans are instinctively grandiose.' (By 'grandiose' he meant 'loud and stupid'.)

But, superbly, there is an agreement in international law that no one can exploit the moon for private gain. Yes: the moon is a common treasury for everyone to share. The moon is socialist.

The UN-sponsored 1979 Agreement Governing the Activities of States on the Moon and Other Celestial Bodies, commonly known as the Moon Treaty, literally forbids the exploitation of the moon. This came about because basically there was no danger of anyone sharing this particular treasury. If it looks like anyone can share this particular treasury, let's see how long the agreement lasts. The smart money is on 'seconds'. No wonder the Belgians are so gung-ho for getting up there. (The imperialist bastards.)

Some people are already trying to get a slice of the moon's action, agreement or no agreement. British-based Richard Garriott bought a long-lost Soviet-era Russian moon probe in some freaky auction years back. When the Lunokhod 2 rover, lost in 1973, turned up in 2011, Garriott claimed he owned the parts of the moon the probe had passed over. He pretended it was a bit of tongue in cheek, but in an I-mean-it sort of a way. Imagine Richard Garriott at corporation level, and that's the future for the moon. Still, for now, Garriott says he owns the moon. But he doesn't, though.

Meanwhile, a Californian company called TransOrbital is the first commercial outfit to be given permission to fly to the moon. The US authorities say it can go to the moon, as long as it doesn't touch it. It's a metaphor. And also a moon mission.

More in keeping with the moon's communitarian vibe, the Alliance to Rescue Civilization wants to put a DNA bank on the moon. Yes, this group's initials are ARC, which conjures the image of the Old Testament partriarch and prophet Noah in space. ARC envisages a moonbase that will guard the very essence of life. Sounds very noble, except it's obviously just another ruse to go into space: 'Honey, by going on this space trip, in space, I'm actually saving humanity!' 'Yeah, right . . . You said that about fucking Honolulu too. And look what happened then.' 'This won't be like Honolulu . . .'

After the moon, next up is Mars. UK Astronomer Royal Martin Rees is already fretting about an orgy of exploitation on Mars. 'Antarctic-style restraint might be feasible,' he told the British Association for the Advancement of Science festival. 'On the other hand, if the explorers were privately

funded adventurers of free-enterprise, even anarchic dis-
position – the wild west model would be more likely to
prevail.' (Cowboys on Mars: it's already been mooted.)

Mars is also wildly inhospitable – a big rocky fucker
that looks like it should be hot, being red, but is actually
very, very, very cold. And to even think realistically about
exploiting Mars (or just sitting on it for a bit) we'd need
to solve the problems of getting there, and also being able
to stay there, and also getting back from there – which,
combined and also separately, represent significant problems *vis à vis* living on bloody Mars.

Mars is a two to three year round trip. So some bright
sparks have suggested sending old people – that is, people
who might not reasonably expect to come back. (Old
people in space: it's already been mooted.) To make it
more interesting for everyone else, one of these elderly
Martian pioneers should clearly be David Bowie. 'David:
is there life on Mars?' 'No-oh-oh.'

The Russians recently experimented with these aspects
of what it was like being stuck in space by sticking six
men in a container in a Moscow car park for 520 days (the
length of a trip to Mars). The mission was called Mars500,
but could have been called Moscow520, but wasn't. They
even simulated an emergency power failure and a walk
on the Martian surface – in a sandpit (I'm not making that
up) complete with fake boulders.

Is living in space like living in a container? Yes. Although
these brave souls had to cope with a lot more than most
people going to Mars: the pointlessness of being stuck
in a container in Moscow for 520 days. The temptation
to just say, 'Nah, this is bollocks, I'm off' would indeed
be great. The satiation of this temptation would not be

available in space. In space, you cannot just say 'I'm off.' Off where?

Is being in space like being in a container in a car park in Moscow? In a way, yes. Is the problem of being in space the problem of not being able to go outdoors? Yes.

Still, it's good to know they didn't go completely to pieces. On their re-emergence from the car park, the Frenchman Romain Charles missed, perhaps inevitably, 'cheese, wine and a nice crunchy baguette'. (He also missed 'films with Juliette Binoche in them' and letting his dog crap on the pavement.)

For Italian/Colombian astronaut Diego Urbina, meanwhile, the worst aspect of the trip to Mars/ Moscow was having to forgo 'simple things like a blue sky, such as going dancing in the evening – I love doing that.'

Who doesn't? So, there's no dancing in the evening in space – or at least in Moscow.

It's life, pretty much as we know it

Going further than the solar system is hard, but not impossible. The nearest star is 10,000 times further than Neptune. So it's quite a poke.

Nevertheless, there are other worlds out there, and not just any old other worlds – your gassy fireballs and frozen wastes or other inhospitable bobbins. No: if we balls this one up, there are plenty more *Earth-like* planets out there (of varying degrees of Earthiness). E-type planets. Planets where *you* could conceivably survive.

A planet 20 light years away is the first outside our solar system to be declared 'habitable' by scientists. The rocky exoplanet (a planet outside the solar system) Gliese 581d (cool name) meets key requirements for sustaining Earth-like life, including rainfall and possibly even watery oceans. But there could be literally billions more across the Milky Way, say observers. So it's game on.

How Earth-like are these planets really, though? And how far away are they? How much in the way of resources would it take to get there?

And is there life out there? Yes. The existence of extremophiles (organisms living in extreme environments) has only recently been properly appreciated and has opened up the boundaries of what life requires. Extremophiles don't need the sun, they just live on energy from volcanic vents on the ocean floor. It's no kind of life, really. But, crucially, it is life.

Suddenly, notions of the 'Goldilocks Zone' are blown right open. Extremophiles are like a Goldilocks who can take the porridge burning hot, freezing cold, any way it comes. Extreme porridge: they can take it.

This even opens the door to aliens within our own solar system. The ice-encrusted oceans of Saturn's icy moon-planet Europa could be full of oxygen, which would be just as sustainable for life as here. Aliens on Europa might actually be a bit close. From no aliens anywhere, to loads of aliens, really, really close.

The ice is etched with a network of mysterious red lines, which hints at a salty ocean underneath possibly 100 kilometres deep (which is deep, let's face it). That would mean there is more than twice as much life-giving water on Europa as on Earth – in which all kinds of life-forms could be swimming about, coldly, being cold, but actually alive. Shivering, essentially. Okay, Europa is not that close. But even accounting for the fact that Europa feels slightly closer than it actually is on account of being called Europa which is very similar to the word 'Europe' which you can sort of see from Dover, it's close enough for aliens. Voyager 1 went past Europa ages ago, about the time of the New Romantics – so we could well have gone past the aliens. (This conjures the image of Spandau Ballet in space.)

So yes: we could one day be communing with alien life-forms, but the form of those lives would be pondlife. 'How's it going?' 'Oh, you know . . .'

But are there alien civilisations with whom we might make contact? It's a good question, one that was supposedly answered by the Drake Equation – a big load of maths, which basically says: look at all those stars. There are easily a billion planets on which intelligent life-forms might have evolved. So they must have.

If life is universal, then surely so is evolution: you cannot really imagine life surviving when it is not intrinsically being that bothered about surviving. A species' survival does not depend on intelligence; but being able to make rational deductions about your surroundings is, you may have found, a useful enough skill to have developed.

Even on Earth, crows and elephants – creatures on completely different evolutionary branches to primates like us – are on the threshold of where we were about 100,000 years ago. In breaking news, jays have developed a theory of kind – i.e. they are good at thinking what other birds are thinking. Don't worry, they have not just developed this, like, this week (it's more that we have recently discovered that they can do this).

All this indicates that space creatures, if they are there,

should be developing logical intelligence, roughly as we would recognise, all over the shop. It's only logical.

But then crashing up against the Drake Equation comes the Fermi Paradox which responds to the maths behind the Drake Equation by asking: well, where are they then? So between the Equation and the Paradox is a clear Contradiction. It's bad when that happens.

So why aren't they here? If life is so common on Earth, then surely it is common elsewhere. But then, would we not see some trace of all this life? Many have responded that perhaps they prefer to keep quiet. Or maybe we are not listening properly. We ourselves are continually discovering new modes of communication. Maybe we are listening on AM when we should be listening on FM. (Not literally . . . although maybe we should all start listening for aliens on AM radios?)

There is also another theory that alien civilisations, in developing the technological wherewithal, inevitably destroy themselves before they get to the stage where we can see them, that civilisation itself has a built-in obsolescence factor, that the eerie silence is the result of intelligent life-forms inevitably inventing the tools to wipe themselves out. Meaning all life in the universe is essentially pre-programmed to vaporise itself in an orgy of power-hungry revulsion; that when we look up at the heavens, we are really looking up at a colossal battleground involving innumerable intelligent alien life-forms committing violent suicide over and over again obeying some universal law of futility and defeat.

It's a fun and interesting theory that you should definitely share with any nearby children the next time the stars are out.

You will fuck space up and you know you will
Space and the humans: is it going to work? Are we
supposed to carry on exploring our limits? Or are
we supposed to stay on Earth, whence we did come, and
to which we are basically quite well suited?

In the long run, of course, we are all of us, stupid aliens,
clever aliens, stupid humans, fish, all going to face the
inevitable heat death of the universe. As the great Brian
Cox himself (BSc, MSc, PhD, TCOGB) so memorably put
it: 'The cosmos will remain vast and cold and desolate.
There is no way of measuring the passage of time. The
arrow of time has simply ceased to exist. It is an inescap-
able fact of the universe. The entire cosmos will die.'

Yeah, cheers for that Brian. Anyway, Earth will end
before that – when the sun implodes in 5 billion years.
Just get over it. But get over it later, as it's not going to
happen for ages.

So space is all right – let's not get too cynical. But let's
not get carried away either. Carried away into space. There
are lots of problems – like the fact that everything is a
long way away. Like, really, really a long way away. Thus
relying on spacecraft yet to be developed, and people
being put into suspended animation, which we don't know
how to do. And the undeniable kicker that living in space
fucks up your body and makes you mad. (Well, it has to
everyone so far – and, as lately discovered, led to abnor-
malities inside the skull, with eyesight and so on, due to
all the pressure.)

But really: are humans simply meant to be on Earth?
At least for now? The sum total of human time spent in
space, if you added it all together, is less than one human
lifetime. (We only started doing it just over 50 years ago.)

It's as if in the entirety of humanity's existence, there is just one person who knows about space. That's not true as loads of people know about space. But still: think about it.

We've been to the moon the sum total of six times. The first landing explored an area not much larger than a tennis court (to stay in view of the cameras) (and in case the man in the moon jumped out). The six plots visited have varied in size from 'a suburban lot to a small township' – leaving more than 14 million square miles of moon entirely unexplored. Can we even say we've *been* to the moon? Yes, because we have been to the moon. But have we though?

Still people want to treat space as some sort of get out of jail free card: fuck up this planet and just get another one. Like we're moments away from decamping *en masse*. Futurist George Friedman even reckons we could outsource our wars up there, to stop mess on earth.

Yes: it's good to dream. But all this deep space exploration stuff relies on things we have little idea how to do. And anyway, Earth is where we have evolved, and where we function best (if, sadly, not ideally).

According to one academic study, our brain functions are boosted by just seeing *a picture* of a tree. Who studies this shit? But still, there are no trees in space. There aren't even many pictures of trees at the moment.

So maybe we should treat ourselves like children: we shouldn't be allowed another planet until we've learnt how to play with the one we've already got.

We certainly have enough to sort out down here as it is. What with (in a world where billions are short of food and water) biotech companies unleashing genetic mutations across the biosphere, robots coming up out of the sewers, Bill Gates spraying the skies with sulphur, the search engine guys penetrating our very essences, immortal bionic-armed *Übermenschen* taking power . . .

CONCLUSION

Cheer up – it might never happen.